Toward A State Of Esteem

*The Final Report of
the California Task Force
to Promote Self-esteem
and Personal and
Social Responsibility*

Dedication

June 26, 1916—September 10, 1988

To the memory of Virginia Satir, who brought to life the concept of self-esteem, who pioneered new therapies as a result, and who touched people all over the world. Self-esteem was central in her work, and she was central in bringing it to others. Virginia helped inspire the legislation behind the Task Force, and, as a fellow member, her partnership with us was close, active, and irreplaceable.

Publishing Information

Toward a State of Esteem, which is the final report of the California Task Force to Promote Self-esteem and Personal and Social Responsibility, was submitted to the California Legislature in January, 1990, as required by *Government Code* Section 8255. This law was enacted on September 23, 1986, when Governor George Deukmejian signed Assembly Bill 3659, which was authored by Assemblyman John Vasconcellos. The 26 members of the Task Force who developed this report are identified on pages xi and xii; the group was headed by Andrew M. Mecca. Those who made significant contributions to the development of the final report are identified on pages xiii and xiv. Special acknowledgment is extended to Rain Blockley for her editing of the manuscript.

Toward a State of Esteem was prepared for photo-offset production by the staff of the California Department of Education's Bureau of Publications, under the direction of Theodore R. Smith, Editor in Chief, who worked with Robert R. Ball, Executive Director, and Ruta D. Aldridge, Associate Director, of the Task Force's staff. The cover and layout for the document were designed and prepared by Cheryl Shawver McDonald. The photos that appear in the publication were provided by Apple Computer, Wernher Krutein/PHOTOVAULT, Emmett E. Miller, M.D., and Pacific Gas & Electric Co.

Toward a State of Esteem was printed by the Office of State Printing and was distributed in accordance with the provisions of *Government Code* sections 8255 and 11096 and the Library Distribution Act, which means that the document is available through every public library in California.

Any questions regarding the reproduction of this document should be addressed to the Copyright Program Officer, California Department of Education, P.O. Box 944272, Sacramento, CA 94244-2720. However, the readers are advised that the "fair use" provisions of the U.S. Copyright Law permit the reproduction of material from the book for "purposes such as criticism, comment, news reporting, teaching (including multiple copies for classroom use), scholarship, or research."

Copies of this publication are available for $4.25 each, plus sales tax for California residents, from the Bureau of Publications, California Department of Education, P.O. Box 271, Sacramento, CA 95812-0271. The fee covers the cost of processing an order, packaging and shipping the book, and maintaining the necessary inventory of the document. Any questions regarding the processing of orders or the distribution of the document should be directed to the Bureau of Publications at the address cited above or by phoning (916) 445-1260. A partial list of other publications available from the Department of Education appears on the inside back cover, or a complete list may be secured by writing or calling the Bureau of Publications.

Appendixes to the Final Report

The *Appendixes to Toward a State of Esteem* is also available in a separate volume for $4.25 each, plus sales tax for California residents, from the Bureau of Publications, California Department of Education, P.O. Box 271, Sacramento, CA 95812-0271. The nine appendixes, which appear in one volume, include (1) a list of operational programs, by county in California, that offer help in areas related to self-esteem; (2) copies of the legislation that created the Task Force and identified its tasks; and (3) an extensive bibliography on self-esteem and personal and social responsibility, which is composed of (a) programs, projects, and curricula; (b) publications, tapes, and videos; (c) assessment instruments; (d) agencies and organizations; (e) publishers and distributors; and (f) human resources. This 120-page volume of appendixes is also available through the public libraries in California.

ISBN 0-8011-0846-2

Contents

I believe that success begins within a person. People must have confidence and courage to confront the challenges that lie ahead in order to achieve their fullest potential. A sense of self-worth and importance is vital to an individual's success and fulfillment.

—*Governor George Deukmejian, in a letter to*
"The Rising Stars of Lincoln Elementary School"
in Long Beach, California

Appendixes (See note on page iv in the "Publishing Statement" for information on the Appendixes, which appear in a separate volume.)

Speaking for myself and for many of my colleagues, I can confirm that the work of the Task Force is historically unique, and may well be pointing the way to developing a new arsenal of instruments with which to deal with some of the most serious social problems of contemporary civilization, and to better our citizens' capacity to improve our individual and collective well-being.

—*Neil Smelser, Professor of Sociology, University of California, Berkeley, in a letter to Task Force chairperson, Andrew M. Mecca*

**CALIFORNIA TASK FORCE TO
PROMOTE SELF-ESTEEM, and
PERSONAL and SOCIAL RESPONSIBILITY**
1130 K STREET, SUITE 300
SACRAMENTO, CA 95814

January 15, 1990

The Honorable George Deukmejian
Governor of California

The Honorable David A. Roberti
President pro Tempore of the Senate

The Honorable Willie L. Brown
Speaker of the Assembly

The Honorable Kenneth L. Maddy
Minority Leader of the Senate

The Honorable Ross Johnson
Minority Leader of the Assembly

The People of California:

The creation of the California Task Force to Promote Self-esteem and Personal and Social Responsibility has been a bipartisan pioneering effort to reframe social problem solving. Rather than reacting to an epidemic of problems, we have turned to an approach that promotes the greater well being of the individual and society. I believe the enclosed findings and recommendations offer a firm cornerstone for this. This work is our legacy to the people of California, the county task forces, and other states and countries that are now planning or already have formed self-esteem task forces.

The past three years' work has demonstrated that self-esteem may well be the unifying concept to reframe American problem solving. This entails moving to a pro-active strategy which supports the empowerment of individuals and local communities to become more involved in developing appropriate responses to the challenges confronting them. Through this process people nurture the four primary ingredients of self-esteem: a sense of belonging, likability, a feeling of significance, and acknowledgment of hard work.

The report does not offer a "quick fix." Rather it plumbs the depth of these social problems and provides concrete recommendations for addressing them. In addition, exemplary programs are profiled to amplify the fact that there are solutions.

Most important, however, is the realization that "self-esteem" is not some "new age, feel good" approach. Rather it is part and parcel of personal and social responsibility. Government and experts cannot fix these problems for us. It is only when each of us recognizes our individual personal and social responsibility to be part of the solution that we also realize higher "self-esteem."

We look around us and see our world full of many enormous problems. They are problems that a single person, a single family, or a single community cannot always solve. Just as the pace and makeup of our society have become infinitely complex, so have the problems. Like villainous tentacles, crime, unemployment, drug and alcohol abuse, teen pregnancies, educational failure, welfare dependency, and violence have reached into our homes and lives.

In 1960, President John F. Kennedy challenged our nation to marshall the will and technological resources to put humans on the moon in a decade, and we did it! Today our nation is faced with epidemic levels of social problems. Nothing short of the renewal of American initiative that includes citizens of all ages and backgrounds will solve these crises.

Now we approach the end of the twentieth century and face a new millennium, only ten years away. There can be no more exciting time than this. We are the human bridge to this new millennium. A new door is literally opening; a new age is actually arriving, and the part we play in this is exciting and essential.

Self-esteem and personal and social responsibility are many things; in their consideration we may use words like honesty, charity, dignity, faith, intellectual energy, optimism, self-acceptance, courage, and love. But above all these, self-esteem and personal and social responsibility are our legacy. They are what we leave behind to our children; they are what we leave behind as a trace of what we stood for.

On behalf of all the Task Force members and citizens who volunteered so generously to this legacy, we are honored to submit to you our findings and recommendations.

Sincerely,

Andrew M. Mecca, Dr.P.H.
Chairperson
California Task Force to Promote Self-esteem
and Personal and Social Responsibility

REPLY TO:

☐ DISTRICT OFFICE
100 PASEO DE SAN ANTONIO
SAN JOSE, CALIFORNIA 95113
(408) 288-7515

☐ CAPITOL OFFICE
STATE CAPITOL
P.O. BOX 942849
SACRAMENTO, CA 94249-0001
TEL: AREA CODE 916
445-4253

COMMITTEES

EDUCATION
SUBCOMMITTEE ON
POSTSECONDARY EDUCATION
ECONOMIC DEVELOPMENT &
NEW TECHNOLOGIES

Assembly
California Legislature

JOHN VASCONCELLOS
ASSEMBLYMAN, TWENTY-THIRD DISTRICT

CHAIRMAN
COMMITTEE ON WAYS AND MEANS

Friends, *I* welcome you to California's pioneering effort to address the causes and cures of many of the major social ills that plague us all today. We have initiated an historic and hopeful search for a "social vaccine"— and your personal participation is crucial to our ultimate success.

We have made a remarkable beginning. Our California Task Force to Promote Self-esteem and Personal and Social Responsibility has far exceeded my initial expectations. It has already served to legitimate self-esteem as a crucial factor in our lives. We have moved self-esteem from an object of Garry Trudeau's satire to a subject widely and deservedly respected.

My desire to create the Task Force grew out of my experience:

1. My own painful personal struggle—despite repeated successes and achievements in my life—to develop my own self-esteem; and

2. My chairing the Assembly Ways and Means Committee, which prepares our state's annual multibillion-dollar budget—with so much going in too-little, too-late efforts to confine and/or repair our fellow Californians, whose lives are in distress and disrepair. (Details in my Preface in *The Social Importance of Self-Esteem)*

So I found myself wanting to turn our attention to searching out the root causes of our social problems and to addressing them effectively, preventively. In 1984 I first introduced the legislation to create the Task Force. It took three years to get it enacted. Now, barely three more years and our Task Force has generated a statewide—and, recently, a nationwide—movement of states and of persons—to promote healthy self-esteem and personal and social responsibility.

As we approach the twenty-first century, we human beings now— for the first time ever—have it within our power to truly improve our human condition. We can proceed to develop a *social vaccine*. We can outgrow our past failures—our lives of crime and violence, alcohol and drug abuse, premature pregnancy, child abuse, chronic dependence on welfare, and educational failure.

In the 1940s some folks with vision and passion marshalled their faith and resources and ingenuity and unlocked the secrets of the atom. In the 1960s others led and unlocked the secrets of gravity and empowered us humans to enter outer space.

In the 1990s we humans have the opportunity to enter our own inner space. We can unlock the secrets of healthy human development. We in California (often the leading state, often pioneers) followed our passion. With this report we point the way toward a successful effort to truly improve our human condition.

The following report gives ample and encouraging evidence that we are well on our way. The wisdom and the tools are now available to us to really move all Californians (and you elsewhere) individually and as a whole toward a healthier state of self-esteem and personal and social responsibility.

It took the diversity and wisdom and generosity of the 26 committed Californians who constituted our Task Force to lay this remarkable foundation. All of us owe them much. I wholeheartedly congratulate and thank each of them.

The success of our endeavor now depends on each of us. Will we recognize the centrality of self-esteem in our lives? Will we commit ourselves to developing our own self-esteem and modeling it in our relationships with every other person in our lives? It is a cause well worth our personal commitment and participation.

As a beginning, carefully read and digest this report. Incorporate its recommendations in your daily life and all of your relationships. Together we can truly grow more self-esteeming and responsible. Together we can truly make a difference. Together we can make history—better. Let us begin—right now!

Sincerely,

John Vasconcellos

John Vasconcellos
Assemblyman
(Author of the enabling legislation)

> I believe that uniqueness is the key word to self-worth . . . Developing your sense of uniqueness, then, is basic to developing high self-esteem.
>
> —*Virginia Satir, Family Therapist*

The Task Force

The California Task Force to Promote Self-esteem and Personal and Social Responsibility

No man has the right to dictate what other men should perceive, create, or produce, but all should be encouraged to reveal themselves, their perceptions and emotions, and to build confidence in the creative spirit.

—*Ansel Adams, Photographer*

Andrew M. Mecca, Dr.P.H.
Chairperson
San Rafael

Wilbur R. Brantley, M.P.A.
Sacramento

B. David Brooks, Ph.D.
Long Beach

Jack Canfield, M.Ed.
Pacific Palisades

Noemi E. Contreras,
M.S.Ed., D.S.W., Ph.D.
Glendale

Paul Kent Froman, Ph.D.
Los Angeles

Raymond E. Gott, M.P.A.
Whittier

Sue Elizabeth Granger-Dickson, M.S.
Bakersfield

William C. Johnson, M.A.
Shingletown

James Kenshalo, M.S.W., L.C.S.W.
Napa

Mary M. Luke, R.N., M.B.A.
San Francisco

Norma Foster Maddy
Modesto

Emmett E. Miller, M.D.
Menlo Park

Mary Myers, Ph.D.
Fresno

Kenneth W. Ogden, M. Div., Ed.D.
Covina

Connie Palladino, Ph.D.
Palo Alto

Task Force Members
(Continued)

Eunice N. Sato, M.A.
Long Beach

Gerti B. Thomas, M.P.A.
Hayward

David Shannahoff-Khalsa
Del Mar

Linda Wargo
San Luis Obispo

Lynn Silton, M.S.
San Francisco

Virginia Satir (deceased)

Statutory Members

Vivian Gannon
(designee for Clifford Allenby, Secretary of Health and Welfare)

Nicholas Osa
(designee for Joe Sandoval, Secretary of Youth and Adult Corrections)

Susie Lange
(designee for Bill Honig, Superintendent of Public Instruction)

Brian Taugher
(designee for John Van de Kamp, Attorney General)

Ex Officio Members

Art Torres, Senator

John Vasconcellos, Assemblyman

Jean Barnaby
(designee for Senator Art Torres)

Task Force Staff

Robert R. Ball, S.T.D.
Executive Director

Ruta D. Aldridge
Associate Director

Estela Escalanté
Secretary

Acknowledgments

We, the members of the California Task Force to Promote Self-esteem and Personal and Social Responsibility, acknowledge the valuable contributions made by many individuals and organizations who assisted us in fulfilling our mandated responsibilities. The Task Force sincerely appreciates the time and effort of those who prepared and/or presented both public and written testimony. The responses from these citizens, community organizations, and public officials were crucial in gaining a full and up-to-date understanding of the issues before us.

The Task Force is especially grateful to the members of the county task forces who shared their time and talents so fully in grasping the importance of this undertaking and who gave so freely of their time in pursuing mutual objectives. Many of these people gave invaluable assistance in organizing and operating the Task Force's public hearings.

The academic foundations for this report were provided through the commitment and cooperation of Dr. David Gardner, President of the University of California, and many UC faculty and staff: Martin Covington, Susan B. Crockenberg, Harry Kitano, Calvin Moore, Karen Paget, Thomas J. Scheff, Leonard Schneiderman, Rodney Skager, Neil Smelser, and Harry Specht.

The Task Force extends a special thanks to a group of Bay Area facilitators who volunteered hundreds of hours to the Task Force in planning, facilitating, and recording meetings and public hearings. Organized by Cathy DeForest, this group included: Victoria Bain, Karen Buckley, Mary Curran, Adriana Diaz, Anna Ewing, Lisa Faithorn, Jan Felicitas, Sharon Franquemont, Marilyn Gatlin, Mary Gelinas, Sue Gershenson, Anita Gherardi, Peter Gibb, Roger James, Rae Levine, Patty McManus, Barbara Miller, Joyce Reynolds, Barbara Schultz, and Jean Westcott.

The Task Force is indebted to the group of professionals who came at their own expense to compose the Think Tank: Betty Berzon, Yogi Bhajan, Nathaniel Branden, B. David Brooks, Jack Canfield, William Coulson, C. W. Gaffney, Thomas Gordon, Lilia "Lulu" Lopez, George McKenna, Bertie Mo, James Newman, Uvaldo Palomares, M. Scott Peck, Robert Reasoner, George Ruiz, Virginia Satir, Gordon Stokes, Ernest Wu, and John Vasconcellos.

G. Albert Howenstein, Executive Director of the Office of Criminal Justice Planning, and his staff were exemplary hosts to the Task Force, providing the members with office space and dozens of day-to-day services.

Thanks are also extended to the following individuals from the Department of Mental Health in their support of the Task Force: D. Michael O'Conner, Doug Arnold, Debra Lee Freeman, Richard Friday, and Sidney Herndon.

The Task Force is grateful to those persons who, at its request, came to Task Force meetings to present information relative to the legislatively mandated areas of concern: Michelle Borba, Sister Beth Burns, Bill Cleveland, Judith Feldman, Thomas Gordon, Linda Harvey, Mildred Harrison, Everett Jensen, Tim O'Neil, Mariam Rashada, Bob Reasoner, Mary Ellen Rivera, George Solomon, M.D., Sharon Strucker, Lynne Vaughan, and Jann Walton.

Others who contributed significantly to the myriad functions of the Task Force's operations were Amy Abraham, John Aldridge, Brooke Allison, Rain Blockley, Carol Bone, Tim Buckles, Michael Bunzel, Sue Covey, Jane Ellis, Peggy Haigh, Susan Haugen, Anne Kronenberg, Myra Livingston, Vonna Breeze-Martin, Joe Parente, Shirley Purvis, Rich Robinson, Michael Twombly, Marina Villa, and the Task Force's Interim Executive Director, Dick Vittitow.

©1987 Wernher Krutein/PHOTOVAULT

Preface

*T*hough this is the Task Force's final report, it is only a beginning, a substantial and encouraging beginning of an historic effort to discover and address the root causes of our major social concerns. We claim no panacea. We do claim success in initiating this effort. The self-esteem movement is alive and well and developing across our state and nation. It deserves our attention, commitment, and involvement.

California is on the verge of becoming our nation's first state with no racial or ethnic majority. Our greatest challenge, as a state and as a people, is to realize our promise as a truly multicultural democracy.

Our record to date in this regard is not enough. It is clear that progress has been slow, *and* that progress can be made. Every Californian, and every California institution—public and private—must accept responsibility for addressing this challenge now.

This report speaks to you and every Californian—for California includes all of us. With this report we present you a work plan and a call to action. We challenge you and every Californian—individual and institution—to rise to a new level of sensitivity, concern, and action.

Not all our ideas are new. Yet we believe that self-esteem brings new life to them, and to us, and better enables each of us to recognize and encourage and incorporate all of our people—of whatever race, nationality, or ethnicity—into every aspect of California's life and well being.

This final report has been carefully and collaboratively prepared. The report is built around the specific mandates assigned to the Task Force by the enabling legislation. Each mandate took on a dimension of its own, with unexpected findings and a broader scope than originally anticipated.

The introductory section of the report outlines the assignment delivered to us, a synopsis of our findings and recommendations, and a statement of the vision which we see for California as a result of this project.

Succeeding sections build on each other:
- Our definition of self-esteem (on which everything else in the report depends) with commentary
- The key principles for nurturing healthy self-esteem and personal and social responsibility, and, finally

- The recommendations and discussion in the areas of personal and social concern

The report's appendix, which appears in a separate volume, contains what we hope will be helpful lists: the world's most complete bibliography of resources on self-esteem, a listing of program resources available to the public, and a compilation of the contact persons for each of the county task forces.

We thank you for your interest in what has become for us a cause with compelling benefits—for us as individuals, for our families, and for our state. We hope you will want to join with us in pursuing those benefits.

TASK FORCE TO PROMOTE
SELF-ESTEEM AND PERSONAL
AND SOCIAL RESPONSIBILITY

We sow a thought and reap an act;
We sow an act and reap a habit;
We sow a habit and reap a character;
We sow a character and reap a destiny.

—*William Makepeace Thackeray,*
English Novelist

Pacific Gas & Electric Co.

I. Executive Summary

A precise understanding of what we mean when we speak of *self-esteem* is crucial to this entire endeavor. The literature review conducted by the University of California on behalf of the Task Force was hindered by the lack of a generally accepted definition. Furthermore, the common public perception of *self-esteem* as a condition of highly individualistic narcissism has resulted in confusion and misunderstanding.

The Task Force adopted this as its official definition:

> *Appreciating my own worth and importance*
> *and having the character to be accountable for myself*
> *and to act responsibly toward others.*

A full appreciation of the recommendations of the Task Force depends on an understanding of this definition. The basic meanings underlying the definition were expanded in a full discussion called key principles.

Key Principles

To fulfill the legislative mandate to compile research "regarding how healthy self-esteem is nurtured, harmed or reduced, and rehabilitated," the Task Force carefully developed a "Key Principles" document. Organized in sections which correspond to the primary elements in the definition, this document provides practical guidance to those who want a better understanding of self-esteem and how it is nurtured.

"Appreciating our Worth and Importance" involves accepting ourselves, setting realistic expectations, forgiving ourselves and others, taking risks, trusting, and expressing feelings. It also rests on appreciating our creativity, our minds, our bodies, and our spiritual beings.

"Appreciating the Worth and Importance of Others" means affirming each person's unique worth, giving personal attention, and demonstrating respect, acceptance, and support. This principle also means setting realistic expectations, providing a sensible structure, forgiving others, taking risks, appreciating the benefits of a multicultural society, accepting emotional expressions, and negotiating rather than being abusive.

"Affirming Accountability for Ourselves" requires taking responsibility for our decisions and actions, being a person of integrity, understanding and affirming our values, attending to our physical health, and taking responsibility for our actions as parents.

"Affirming our Responsibility Toward Others" means respecting the dignity of being human, encouraging independence, creating a sense of belonging, developing basic skills, providing physical support and safety, fostering a democratic environment, recognizing the balance between freedom and responsibility, balancing cooperation and competition, and serving humanity.

Recommendations and Discussion

The legislation directed the Task Force to make "findings and recommendations applicable to the relevant areas of study. . .that will enhance the broadest possible understanding and appreciation by policymakers and program operators and all Californians. . .". The Task Force's recommendations are, therefore, directed to persons across that broad spectrum of interest, arranged by subjects, and correlated with information about programs that may be contacted and examined as illustrations of the kind of effort being proposed.

The Family

"Family" is first in the sequence of topics because the Task Force came to the unanimous conviction that the family is the most crucial ingredient in nurturing the sense of self-esteem persons carry with them into life. This decisive influence is explained in the discussion portion of this section.

Because parents are so crucial to self-esteem and responsibility in our society, steps need to be taken to assist them in fulfilling their critical tasks. This will include workshops for those who are now carrying the responsibility of being parents and classes to prepare young people for this awesome assignment. Learning good parental techniques is important, but the self-esteem of the parents themselves is, by far, the most crucial and essential element!

Education and Academic Failure

If the family is the first in importance in nurturing self-esteem, the schools are second. More than in any other single area of our study, schools have demonstrated the centrality of self-esteem. Schools that deliberately nurture self-esteem have recorded impressive results in academics as well as in social and personal responsibility.

The Task Force is recommending that every school district make a conscious effort to promote self-esteem and personal and social responsibility. Because good education requires good self-esteem, the Task Force recommends that training in this area be a part of the teacher credentialing process and a part of all in-service training.

Drug and Alcohol Abuse

The statistics on drug and alcohol abuse and the myriad other problems related to them are staggering and getting worse. Though substance abuse is too complex a concern to be tied to any one causal agent, the data are clear that low self-esteem is a significant contributing factor. It is also evident that enhancing self-esteem so as to affect abusive behavior requires a deep change in one's sense of self. Difficult though it will be, this reducing-the-demand approach holds great promise for long-term benefits.

The Task Force was impressed with the ability of communities to deal with their own drug and alcohol abuse problems and recommends the development of local prevention councils. We need to support families, schools, and successful treatment programs. The Task Force also calls on the media to accept responsibility for its part in shaping public self-esteem and especially for its presentation of acceptable behavior with regard to the use of drugs and alcohol.

Crime and Violence

When young people fail to find acceptance and affirmation, a sense of belonging, and a significant part in decision making, many of them seek those human necessities in gangs. People need to know that they matter—to be able to experience the personal accomplishment of making a difference. When these opportunities are not available in positive endeavors and relationships, disappointed and frustrated people often pursue them in ways that are both personally and socially destructive. We need, therefore, to encourage and equip families, schools, and communities to promote opportunities for self-esteem and responsible behavior.

We also need to make self-esteem and responsibility training a part of the state's penal and criminal justice systems. Accepting responsibility for the consequences of one's own decisions and behavior is an integral part of healthy self-esteem. The Task Force, therefore, encourages the juvenile justice system to develop consistent and appropriate penalties for every criminal act. Just as families benefit from allowing their children to experience the consequences of their choices and behavior, so does society.

Poverty and Chronic Welfare Dependency

The Task Force found that being a welfare recipient can be destructive to self-esteem, encourages a "learned helplessness," and undermines one's efforts to be personally and socially responsible. Assistance programs, therefore, must be sensitive to every person's need for dignity and respect. This emphasis needs to include both recipients and the staff who work with them. All aid programs need to help people move toward high self-esteem and financial self-sufficiency.

Welfare recipients often need training in vocational and educational opportunities, independent living skills, and interpersonal communications.

The Workplace   Although the workplace was not an area assigned in the enabling legislation, through public hearings it became evident to the Task Force that it had to take note of the critical influence of the workplace on self-esteem and responsible living. Corporate policies and procedures have a crucial impact on the sense of dignity, worth, and responsibility felt by employees. Employers must, therefore, be sensitive to these areas of concern and be willing to recognize the special needs of their employees as human beings, family members, and parents. Businesses also have a responsibility to the community and can assist in resolving social concerns. This can happen only in an environment of mutual esteem.

Appendix to the Report

As a supplement to our report, the Appendix includes what we think to be the largest bibliography of self-esteem resource materials to be found in the world, a listing of self-esteem program resources, an outline of the work being done by the various county task forces, and copies of the legislation relevant to this enterprise. Because of the size of the Appendix, we chose to place it in a separate volume. (See the publishing statement on page iv for information on ordering a copy of the Appendix.)

Key Findings

• Self-esteem is the likeliest candidate for a *social vaccine*, something that empowers us to live responsibly and that inoculates us against the lures of crime, violence, substance abuse, teen pregnancy, child abuse, chronic welfare dependency, and educational failure. The lack of self-esteem is central to most personal and social ills plaguing our state and nation as we approach the end of the twentieth century.

Emmett E. Miller, M.D.

- The family is the incubator of self-esteem and the most crucial social unit in a child's life and development. The early months and years of a child's life are the most decisive in establishing a solid base for authentic, abiding self-esteem and depth of personal character.
- The parent's high self-esteem is vital to his or her ability to provide a healthy environment for the child. We need to extend great effort to assist parents to develop their own self-esteem and to become more knowledgeable, capable, and effective in nurturing children's positive self-esteem and personal responsibility.
- Since children spend so much of their time in school, the environment of the school also plays a major role in the development of self-esteem. Schools that feature self-esteem as a clearly stated component of their goals, policies, and practices are more successful academically as well as in developing healthy self-esteem.
- Experiencing our spiritual side is part of being human. Nourishing our spirit is necessary if we want healthy self-esteem.
- Every person is potentially creative, and appreciating our creativity is crucial for healthy self-esteem.
- Young people who are self-esteeming are less likely to become pregnant as teenagers.
- People who esteem themselves are less likely to engage in destructive and self-destructive behavior, including child abuse, alcohol abuse, abuse of other drugs (legal and illegal), violence, crime, and so on. Without discounting the importance of those early years, people can achieve healthier self-esteem at any age. So information and opportunities for choosing to do so must be made available to citizens of all ages and circumstances. Again, it is not simply new knowledge that we need, but a new awareness of ourselves as we experience new kinds of affirmation and acceptance.
- Regardless of age, race, creed, sex, or sexual orientation, an affirming environment in the home, school, workplace, and community is crucial for nurturing self-esteem. This is a personal and public responsibility that we need to recognize, accept, and undertake. The choice to esteem ourselves is also a decision for which each of us, ultimately, is personally responsible, no matter what our backgrounds may have been.

Key Recommendations

The Family, Teenage Pregnancy, and Child Abuse

1. Develop a statewide media campaign to educate all Californians regarding the primary role of parents in the development of healthy self-esteem and of personal and social responsibility; and provide appropriate, culturally sensitive multilingual training in loving and effective ways to raise children.

2. The Legislature should recognize the profound and primary role of parents by funding and directing the State Department

of Education to implement culturally sensitive and age-appropriate courses in parenting for students throughout their educational experience.

Education and Academic Failure

1. Every school district in California should adopt the promotion of self-esteem and of personal and social responsibility as a clearly stated goal, integrated into its total curriculum and informing all of its policies and operations.

   School boards should establish policies and procedures that value staff members and students and serve to foster mutual respect, esteem, and cooperation.

2. Course work in self-esteem should be required for credentials and as a part of ongoing in-service training for all educators.

Drugs and Alcohol Abuse

1. Local officials should develop community-based substance abuse prevention councils that, in addition to overseeing local prevention efforts, simultaneously promote self-esteem and personal and social responsibility.

2. Expand and support treatment programs for substance abusers by replicating successful programs.

Crime and Violence

1. Establish a juvenile justice system that will develop personal responsibility in juvenile offenders by consistently imposing appropriate sanctions for every criminal act.

2. Support the replication of successful community-based juvenile delinquency prevention programs that foster respect, positive self-esteem, and personal and social responsibility.

Poverty and Chronic Welfare Dependency

1. Support and implement programs that assist long-term welfare recipients to grow in self-esteem and responsibility so they can move from the welfare rolls to independence.

2. Encourage and aid assistance programs, such as AFDC, to enable single parents to establish nurturing home environments by providing optional services, such as training for effective parenting, independent living skills, educational and vocational counseling, and child-care options.

The Workplace

1. Encourage the development of personnel policies and working conditions that promote self-esteem and personal and social responsibility in both the private and public sectors.

2. Public and private industry should institute policies to meet the changing needs of the American family; for example, jobsite child care, flextime work schedules, job sharing, and parental leave. Employers should be encouraged to implement programs, policies, and practices that ensure an esteeming environment for workers and their families.

Recommendations in Brief Form

The Family, Teenage Pregnancy, and Child Abuse

1. Highlight the important role of parents through a media campaign.
2. Include child-rearing courses in the school curriculum.
3. Make courses on child rearing available to all.
4. Make self-esteem-enhancing child care available to all.
5. Provide health education for expectant mothers and fathers.
6. Provide self-esteem and responsibility training for all foster parents and institutional-care staff.
7. Reduce the number of teenage pregnancies through self-esteem training.
8. Provide family life programs for adolescents.
9. Provide programs to encourage responsibility of teenage fathers.
10. Provide support programs for parents at risk of abusing children.
11. Provide women's shelters that contain a self-esteem and responsibility component.

Education and Academic Failure

1. Self-esteem and responsibility must be woven into the total education program.
2. Educate every educator through pre-service and in-service training in self-esteem and responsibility.
3. Give students opportunities to do community service.
4. Formulate a real-life skills curriculum.
5. Promote more parent involvement.
6. Be sensitive to the needs of students at risk of failure.
7. Use the arts to help develop self-esteem and responsibility.
8. Expand counseling and peer counseling services for students.
9. Provide cooperative learning opportunities.
10. Reduce class size or student: adult ratios.
11. Implement programs to counteract bigotry and prejudice.

Drugs and Alcohol Abuse

1. Create prevention councils in every community.
2. Expand treatment programs.
3. Create culturally sensitive prevention strategies.
4. Educate parents.
5. Expand school prevention programs.
6. Encourage responsible media.

Crime and Violence

1. Hold juveniles accountable for crime.
2. Replicate programs that foster self-esteem and responsibility.
3. Combat gangs with self-esteem programs in schools.
4. Create community partnerships to develop after-school activities.

5. Establish self-esteem programs in correctional facilities.
6. Develop self-esteem programs for criminal justice agencies.
7. Provide self-management and coping skills for inmates.
8. Promote arts programs in institutional settings.
9. Establish community correctional facilities.

Poverty and Chronic Welfare Dependency

1. Support programs that assist long-terms welfare recipients towards independence.
2. Encourage programs that provide parents with the tools to be good parents.
3. Encourage programs that establish peer support groups.
4. Provide in-service self-esteem training to staff who work with welfare recipients.
5. Implement welfare reform programs that alter attitudes and enhance motivation.
6. Provide incentives for communities and businesses to work together to promote youth programs.

The Workplace

1. Promote affirming workplace environments.
2. Provide employer support for employee/parents and families.
3. Encourage more businesses to get involved in their communities.

No one can give self-esteem to anyone else. We can provide a supportive environment for personal growth, opportunities for successful experiences in goal-directed behavior, and productive roles for all citizens.

—*Mary Mallory, Ph.D., California State University, Fresno*

Pacific Gas & Electric Co.

II. The Task Force's Vision and Recommended Action

Daring to Dream

Only when we dare to dream—to build a vision—can we improve our world.

In 1776 a handful of visionaries dreamed of freedom, of a democratic society, of a government of the people and by the people and for the people. Because they dared to dream, it happened.

In 1961 President John F. Kennedy dared to dream the impossible: to put a man on the moon within ten years. His vision led the way, and many Americans committed themselves and made it happen.

Today, many Californians have a new vision to build a society in which self-esteem is nurtured and people naturally assume personal and social responsibility.

The vision has already begun to come true. Local task forces have been formed in 46 of our state's 58 counties because many Californians have dared to dream. And with this report we reach forward in our hopes of extending this dream into the twenty-first century.

We invite you to join us as we envision the following possibilities. Stretch your imagination into the future, beyond presently accepted limits. Some of these possibilities will become a reality by the year 2000.

There is no beginning too small.

—*Henry David Thoreau*

It is only with the heart that the mind sees clearly.

—*Antoine de Saint-Exupéry, French Writer*

In the twenty-first century we Californians will have integrated the principles of self-esteem and of personal and social responsibility into our personal lives and into our families, businesses, governments, and communities.

Families

In the twenty-first century, families of all types are recognized and operating as the primary source for modeling self-esteem and personal and social responsibility.

Children are welcomed into the world by parents who esteem themselves and who appreciate and support their children's natural tendencies toward becoming constructive, responsible, and trustworthy.

Children are nurtured by their parents in such a way that they all become healthy individuals who have a sense of identity and an awareness of their own worth and potential.

Feelings of worth can flourish only in an atmosphere where individual differences are appreciated, mistakes are tolerated, communication is open, and rules are flexible—the kind of atmosphere that is found in a nurturing family.

—*Virginia Satir, Family Therapist*

Through widespread parental education, parents develop a deeply felt sense of their own worth, a knowledge of the nature and developmental stages of their children, and an appreciation of positive, healthy, and effective ways to be parents.

Families provide every member with healthy, stimulating, informative, and growth-producing experiences.

Education

In the twenty-first century, self-esteem and personal and social responsibility are integral parts of the lifelong learning process.

Schools welcome and support children, regardless of sex, race, nationality, creed, or socioeconomic status. Students are seen as precious and deserving of recognition and attention.

Schools provide rich educational experiences that are designed to:
* Awaken the learner in each student.
* Develop each child's learning capacity and appreciation for learning as a lifelong experience.
* Provide an education that appreciates the uniqueness of each child.
* Address the special needs of every student.
* Serve to liberate rather than domesticate.
* Promote responsible character and values.
* Provide children with role models, experiences, and skills necessary to develop their creativity, intuition, and imagination.

Schools are operated by administrators and teachers who have experienced self-esteem education, who esteem themselves, and who are valued by their communities and by the system they work for. They are sensitive to and comfortable with students of all races and learning styles, they know how to teach students to esteem themselves, and they are positive role models.

School curricula reflect the richness of California's cultural diversity.

Schools provide children with peer counseling and cooperative learning experiences.

Every student is prepared to become fully competent in the six R's: Reading, 'Riting, and 'Rithmetic—and Responsibility, self-Respect, and Relationships.

Businesses and governments work together to provide opportunities for people to develop marketable skills.

Let everything you do be done as if it makes a difference.

—William James

Communities

People in the twenty-first century recognize self-esteem and personal and social responsibility as bridges of acceptance for all ethnic groups and cultural, spiritual, and service organizations.

California is the world's foremost multicultural democracy.

Our communities have become living laboratories in healthy human relations and development, miniature multicultural democracies. Our entire state has become a learning-oriented community.

Californians are respectful of all persons, regardless of sex, race, color, creed, age, or sexual orientation.

Healthy communities and healthy individuals stimulate and reinforce each other.

Community citizens provide themselves a healthy and safe environment. Crime, violence, homelessness, and drug addiction are vanishing in the face of the *social vaccine* of self-esteem.

Californians have developed healthy, effective, and nonviolent ways of resolving conflicts and disputes.

As key and influential components of communities, the media practice their commitment to feature and model responsible behavior and to help build self-esteem among all the members of their communities.

When we are really honest with ourselves, we must admit that our lives are all that really belong to us. So it is how we use our lives that determine what kind of (people) we are.

—*César Chavez to Robert Kennedy*

Pacific Gas & Electric Co.

Businesses

In the twenty-first century, self-esteem and personal and social responsibility are integral parts of our corporate culture.

Businesses operate with the joint goals of productivity and social responsibility. They seek healthy balances among human, economic, and environmental issues.

California industry values the environment and actively seeks nonpolluting alternatives.

The workplace environment and training programs nurture self-esteem. This has resulted in higher productivity and markedly reduced absenteeism.

The California economy is competitive, leading the Pacific Rim developments.

Businesses are owned and managed by persons who esteem themselves and who seek to develop in their employees self-esteem, leadership, and creativity.

All persons are treated equally and respectfully in the workplace, regardless of sex, race, color, creed, age, or sexual orientation. Californians are actively developing their self-esteem and increasing their productivity.

It is inherently easier to develop a negative argument than to advance a constructive one.

—*John Steinbeck*

In the twenty-first century every government level in the state and each of its programs are designed to empower people to become self-realizing and self-reliant. Each promotes self-esteem and personal and social responsibility.

Every citizen (and noncitizen as well) recognizes his or her personal responsibility for fully engaging in the political process, and he or she recognizes the possibility for positively affecting every other person in every situation and relationship.

We are governed by responsible elected and appointed persons, who esteem themselves and have the integrity and competence to lead our people well. Our leaders approach decisions and problems in a universally and systematically inclusive and collaborative manner.

Every level of government participates in a full-scale public sector–private sector partnership and has earned the confidence of our people.

We, the members of the California Task Force to Promote Self-esteem and Personal and Social Responsibility, believe California has the potential for this kind of future. This is the challenge we now place before all Californians. This is the hope and promise of this report and of all Californians actively promoting self-esteem and personal and social responsibility.

Taking Action

What can you do, personally, to promote self-esteem and personal and social responsibility?

You may want to act on your own right now, and we of the Task Force encourage you to do so. Or you may want to learn more before designing a personal plan of action. Reading the section of this report called "Key Principles for Nurturing Healthy Self-esteem and Personal and Social Responsibility" is a good place to start. Other sections of our report may also interest you, and our bibliography may lead to other publications that speak directly to your particular interests, talents, and concerns.

Another beginning is simply to reach out to others who feel as you do. Being with people who value themselves and each other does more than bring us pleasure; it strengthens our own feelings of self-esteem and inspires us to encourage it in others.

Where can you find people like this? You may already know them. Perhaps they are your supportive friends, coworkers, or people you spend time with regularly. You may meet them at the gym, in a class, in connection with your child's preschool play group, or when you take part in community efforts. Use our report as a way to start a conversation.

You may want to reach out to meet new people as well. Taking a parents' class at a local college or volunteering for some special project can bring you in contact with others who share your feelings. Support groups, parents' groups, and Alcoholics Anonymous or Al-Anon are likewise good opportunities for exploring how changes in your sense of worth affect your daily life.

Self-esteem has to do with our reputation with our "selves." So, one way or another, that's where we all must begin—by taking responsibility for ourselves, choosing how well to treat ourselves. Sometimes it helps to gain insight into the destructive influences that have given us negative images of ourselves, but there is no benefit in stopping there and blaming others for our low self-esteem. To take responsibility for raising our own self-worth represents our commitment to health, wholeness, and responsible living.

As we grow in our own self-esteem, we are able to assist others in their growth. When any member of a family begins to feel more positively about himself or herself, the atmosphere in that home changes. We cannot give high self-esteem to anyone, but we can help create an affirming environment in which people can more realistically choose to esteem themselves. Doing so also represents our taking personal responsibility for living our commitment, putting it into action in our daily lives and relationships.

The future belongs to those who believe in their dreams.

—*Eleanor Roosevelt*

©1988 Wernher Krutein/PHOTOVAULT

The same is true in the wider communities of which we are all a part—neighborhoods, schools, workplaces, professional societies, and social, service, political, and religious groups. When we act on the conviction that all human beings, including ourselves, deserve to be treated with dignity and respect, we create a new environment of health and growth and community. Even one such person can open the way for another person to choose to move from the futility of despair to hopeful responsibility, from self-hatred to self-love, from fear and mistreatment of others to a life of inclusiveness, appreciation, and respect.

In the final analysis, changing the way we treat ourselves and each other depends on you, on your commitment and action, far more than on our Task Force. We have initiated this effort and hope it serves to make the promotion of self-esteem and personal and social responsibility visible and central as a public issue. Only you can bring it all to life.

The names, addresses, and information listed below have been supplied to the State Task Force by counties in order to facilitate the location of county task forces by interested Californians.

Alameda
Jill L'Esperance
Social Services Department
401 Broadway
Oakland, CA 94607
(415) 268-2100

Alpine
Kathy Hartzell
Box 4
Markleeville, CA 96120
(916) 694-2194

Amador
John Halverson
Amador Unified School District
217 Rex Avenue
Jackson, CA 95642
(209) 223-1750

Butte
Amber Palmer
853 Manzanita Court
Chico, CA 95926
(916) 891-1731

Calaveras
Gary Duda
P.O. Box 1198
Arnold, CA 95223
(209) 795-1155

Colusa
Amber Palmer
853 Manzanita Court
Chico, CA 95926
(916) 891-1731

Contra Costa
George Johnson
Human Services Advisory
   Commission
Inventory Work Group
2425 Bisso Lane, Suite 103
Concord, CA 94520
(415) 646-5661

Del Norte
Mick Miller
Department of Mental Health
Crescent City, CA 95531
(707) 464-7224

El Dorado
Al Burlingame
2831 Gardella Lane
Camino, CA 95709
(916) 644-3845

Fresno
Pat Imperatrice
1601 West Fairmont, #B
Fresno, CA 93705
(209) 226-1966

Glenn
Pat Ireland
1333 W. Sycamore St., #25
Willows, CA 95988
(916) 934-5416

Humboldt
Bonnie Neely
825 5th Street
Eureka, CA 95501-1172
(707) 445-7471

Imperial
Letty Groom
1398 Sperber Road
El Centro, CA 92243
(619) 339-6402

Inyo
Jim Snead
P.O. Box 1046
Bishop, CA 93513
(619) 872-1104 (work)
(619) 873-4966 (home)

Kern
Gigi Sorenson
2420 Pine Street
Bakersfield, CA 93301
(805) 322-1021

One of my treasures is my list of persons and organizations whose contributions have made life better for all of us. To my list is added this Task Force, whose daring idea of promoting self-esteem is spreading across our nation. What greater virtue than to help people live with more confidence?

—*Al Burlingame, Chairperson
El Dorado County Task Force*

Kings
Nick Kenney
Government Center
1400 W. Lacey Blvd.
Hanford, CA 93230
(209) 582-3211

Lake
No contact person/group at this time.

Lassen
Jim Chapman
Courthouse
Susanville, CA 96130
(916) 257-8311

Los Angeles
Jim Newman
P.O. Box 1994
Studio City, CA 91604
(213) 877-7800

Madera
Audrey Pool
108 Mainberry Drive
Madera, CA 93637

Marin
Jim Shipley
P.O. Box 4925
San Rafael, CA 94913
(415) 868-2611

Mariposa
Supervisor Arthur Baggett
P.O. Box 784
Mariposa, CA 95338
(209) 966-3222

Mendocino
Tom McMillan
1900 Mooswood
Ukiah, CA 95482
(707) 468-3123
Doug Strong
1900 Mooswood
Ukiah, CA 95482
(707) 463-2437

Merced
Nancy Mengenbier
Department of Mental Health
650 West 19th
Merced, CA 95340
(209) 385-6945

Modoc
No contact person/group at this time.

Mono
Tom Wallace
P.O. Box 1176
Mammoth Lakes, CA 93546
(619) 934-8648

Monterey
Katrina Ognyanovich
P.O. Box 7125
Carmel, CA 93921
(408) 373-1493

Napa
Suzanne Shiff
P.O. Box 10031
Napa, CA 94581
(707) 257-7835

Nevada
Charlotte Bollinger
c/o Board of Supervisors
P.O. Box 6100
Nevada City, CA 95959
(916) 265-3211 (work)
(916) 273-6442 (home)

Orange
No contact person/group at this time, although previously there had been a large grass roots organization.

Placer
Tad Kitada
Placer County Office of
    Education
360 Nevada Street
Auburn, CA 95603
(916) 889-8020 ext. 6726

Plumas
Bob Douglas
P.O. Box 10330
Quincy, CA 95971
(916) 283-2200

Riverside
Aletrice Martin
P.O. Box 868
3939 Thirteenth Street
Riverside, CA 95202
(714) 788-6602

Sacramento
Mary Ellen Rivera
County Self-Esteem Liaison
County Office of Education
9738 Lincoln Village Drive
Sacramento, CA 95827
(916) 366-4370

San Benito
Mike Sanchez
San Andreas School
191 Alverado
Hollister, CA 95023
(408) 637-9269

San Bernardino
Kent Paxton
Department of Public Social
    Services
468 W. Fifth Street, Suite 110
San Bernardino, CA 92415-0510
(714) 387-8966

San Diego
Norma Colunga
Supervisor Leon Williams
1600 Pacific Highway, MS-A500
San Diego, CA 92101
(619) 531-5865

San Francisco
Frank Siccone
City Hall, Room 245
San Francisco, CA 94102
(415) 922-2244

Tressa Chambers-Myers
436 Goldmine Drive
San Francisco, CA 94131
(415) 821-6334

San Joaquin
LaDonna Johnson
County Administrator's
    Office
222 East Webber, Room 207
Stockton, CA 95202
(209) 944-2111

San Luis Obispo
Linda Shepard
County Office of Education
P.O. Box 8105
San Luis Obispo, CA 93402
(805) 543-7732

San Mateo
George Riley
401 Marshall Street
Redwood City, CA 94063
(415) 363-4221

Santa Barbara
Charlene A. Chase
Department of Social Services
117 E. Carrillo
Santa Barbara, CA 93101
(805) 568-3200

Santa Clara
Cecelia Arroyo
Santa Clara County Self-
    Esteem
Office of County Executive
70 West Hedding, E. Wing,
    11th floor
San Jose, CA 95110
(408) 299-4714

Santa Cruz
Lynn C. Miller
McDowell Youth Homes, Inc.
P.O. Box 1086
Aptos, CA 95001-1086
(408) 688-8697

Shasta
Karen S. Frost
1644 Magnolia Ave.
Redding, CA 96001
(916) 244-4600

Sierra
Donald McIntosh
P.O. Box 504
Downieville, CA 95936
(916) 289-3194

Siskiyou
LeRoy Foster
P.O. Box 65
Mt. Shasta, CA 96067
(916) 926-5620

Solano
Lee Sturn-Simmons
321 Tuolumne Street
Vallejo, CA 94590
(707) 553-5363

Sonoma
Kate Jenkins
CHDC
2462 Mendocino Avenue
Santa Rosa, CA 95403
(707) 523-1155

Stanislaus
Annarae Luevano
118 North Avenue
Turlock, CA 95380
(209) 667-0885

Sutter
Richard Empey
1025 Teesdale Road
Yuba City, CA 95991
(916) 674-2261

Tehama
Steven R. Chamblin
Tehama County Department
  of Education
P.O. Box 689
1135 Lincoln Street
Red Bluff, CA 96080
(916) 527-5811

Tuolumne
Gloria Dunn
P.O. Box 879
Tuolumne, CA 95379
(209) 928-4826

Trinity
Robert C. Kausen
State Route 2-3968
Trinity Center, CA 96091
(916) 266-3235

Tulare
Mary Louise Vivier
Kaweah Delta District
  Hospital
400 W. Mineral King
Visalia, CA 93291
(209) 625-7241

Ventura
Angie Varela
Supervisor John Flynn
800 S. Victoria Avenue
Ventura, CA 93009
(805) 654-2706

Yolo
Sandi Redenbach
313 Del Oro Avenue
Davis, CA 95616
(916) 666-0264 (work)
(916) 756-8678 (home)

Yuba
Howard Hayes
Yuba City Superinten-
  dent of Schools
938 14th Street
Marysville, CA 95901
(916) 633-2473 (work)
(916) 741-6231 (home)

III. The Definition of Self-esteem

Self-esteem Defined

Appreciating my own worth and importance and having the character to be accountable for myself and to act responsibly toward others.

After extensive testimony and months of deliberations, the Task Force adopted the above definition of self-esteem, especially as it relates to personal and social responsibility.

The effort to define self-esteem is useful, both to bring clarity in our own thinking and to allow understanding in communication.

Each of us has an inner sense of what self-esteem is, but surprises await anyone who reviews the variety of definitions that have been used by thoughtful persons in the field.

Even greater surprises are in store for those who debate with others the best phrase to describe self-esteem. Different aspects of self-esteem are more important to some than others. Our notions are colored by our own experiences.

For some, self-esteem is the conscious appreciation of our own worth and importance, the reputation we have with ourselves. For others, the need to be responsible for ourselves and to act responsibly toward others is paramount.

The California Task Force to Promote Self-esteem and Personal and Social Responsibility invested considerable energy in exploring these meanings. We discovered that some researchers included in their definition of self-esteem what we regard as its polar opposite, namely, a false, vain, and narcissistic preoccupation with oneself which prevents a healthy self-esteem.

These comments are designed to enlarge on our definition and to distinguish between healthy self-esteem and self-glorification.

> Tell me, and I'll forget.
> Show me, and I may not remember.
> Involve me, and I'll understand.
>
> —*Native American Saying*

Commentary on the Definition

"Appreciating my own worth and importance . . ."

To appreciate my own worth and importance means to be aware of and to recognize the significance of my inherent worth, of my value to myself and to others, of my place in the world.

Being alive as a human being has an innate importance, an importance to which the authors of Declaration of Independence referred when they declared that all people "are endowed by their Creator with certain unalienable rights . . .." This conviction concerning the dignity of every human personality has long been a part of our nation's moral and religious heritage. Every person has unique significance, simply because the precious and mysterious gift of life as a human being has been given. This is an inherent value which no adversary or adversity can take away.

This sense of innate worth is reinforced when each individual's unique abilities are recognized, developed, and used to enrich our society. The more we recognize, explore, and develop these abilities, the more we appreciate our own worth and importance.

Achieving more and more of our own potential and recognizing our achievements act in important ways to enhance our self-esteem. The competence that comes with developing skills helps us to deal with life as it presents itself to us, reaffirming our own worth and importance in the midst of whatever experiences come our way.

Appreciating my own worth and importance does not depend on measuring the quantity or quality of my abilities against those of someone else. Every person's abilities are valuable and needed. Each of us has a contribution to make to our society. The more our abilities are developed for the benefit of ourselves and others, the fuller our lives and the richer the world will be.

Appreciating is more than simple recognition. Appreciating means to cherish, to treasure, to respect, and to enjoy my innate and developed worth. This positive personal attitude toward life and the persons around me continually deepens the foundation of my self-esteem.

This is the kind of pride that arises from healthy self-regard, based on a realistic grasp of my own strengths and weaknesses. It is not the same as *false pride* or pseudo self-esteem, an all too common condition in which vanity and arrogance overshadow a person's true self and identity, masking shame about myself.

As I come to a fuller appreciation of my own worth, I grow in confidence, in my sense of adequacy, and in my capability to live responsibly and effectively. This personal growth contributes to an emotional and spiritual warmth which becomes part of my sense of myself and my relationship with others.

Today responsibility is often meant to denote duty, something imposed upon one another from the outside. But responsibility, in its true sense, is an entirely voluntary act; it is my response to the needs, expressed or unexpressed, of another human being.

—Erich Fromm, Psychotherapist

". . . and having the character to be accountable for myself"

Appreciating my own worth and importance is futile if it fails to foster responsible character and integrity in my actions. Character needs to be nurtured. It proceeds from a healthy sense of myself and, like any living entity, it needs to be nourished.

For human beings growth is always possible. As long as we are alive as human beings, we are growing, moving toward more wholeness of character and greater integrity of behavior.

Character is evidenced in actions, in a set of values by which we deal with ourselves and others in a consistently respectful way. Our actions reveal what is important to us. Honesty, compassion, discipline, industriousness, reverence, perseverance, devotion, forgiveness, kindness, courage, gratitude, and grace are among the qualities which integrity of character produces.

Character is nurtured in the family that loves and accepts the child, thus affirming his or her worth and importance. Persons so nurtured are freed from the impossible burden of trying to *prove* their worth and value. They are released to be who they really are: loved and loving human beings.

Every child needs to be treated with respect, consistently, and from the earliest moments of life.

There is no fully adequate substitute for a loving family as the environment in which people learn to appreciate their own worth. There are, however, other important nurturing communities (such as schools, churches, and the workplace) that can provide support to help build integrity of character and self-esteem.

Integrity of character must also be nurtured within ourselves. We must learn to prize our uniqueness, to affirm our worth, to appreciate our significance, to stand for ourselves, and to remind ourselves to our value in the communities that nurture us.

A well-nurtured character combines with an appreciation of one's own worth and importance to foster a healthy, productive citizen.

"... to be accountable for myself"

Being accountable means accepting responsibility for my own actions, for the consequences of my own behavior. The sensibility we bring to our health through diet and exercise is also an example of being accountable.

Too often responsibility is harsh when imposed from the outside; but when personal accountability arises from a personal inner choice, we are freed from confusion and self-deception.

Persons who are accountable for themselves value their own worth as capable, choice-making persons. They do not look to others to create their happiness, and they do not blame others for their sorrows. They accept responsibility for their own lives, not accusing others of preventing their fulfillment; and, insofar as it is possible, they take care of themselves.

Persons who are accountable for themselves do not live thoughtless, haphazard lives. They deliberately choose the values and standards by which they live. They learn from failures, finding opportunities to learn and grow.

"... and to act responsibly toward others"

The more we appreciate our own worth and importance, the more we are able to recognize and appreciate the worth and importance of others as well. As we grow as unique persons, we learn to respect the uniqueness of others and to appreciate the value of our differences.

We are all human beings, yet we express ourselves differently in terms of our individual and cultural diversity. Acting responsibly toward others moves us to accept those differences—to recognize other people's rights to choose for themselves and to be accountable for their own behavior.

Yet simple awareness is not enough. A true appreciation of the worth of others will lead us to action, to deeds through which we treat others with dignity and respect.

The primary way in which we show respect to others is to step out of the state of anxious self-concern long enough to give others our attention—to listen, to understand, to care.

Valuing the significance of being human prompts us to reach out to other human beings in need, to value and support those institutions and rights on which the opportunity to be authentically human depends, such as the home, each person's individual and cultural heritage, our democratic government, and an appreciated, healthy, growing environment.

Responsible action has a personal dimension, moving each one of us to find respectful ways to deal with other members of our families, our friends, our colleagues and customers, the strangers we meet on the street, and human beings around the world.

Responsible action is also corporate. We all belong to groups and institutions which interact with other groups and institutions. As members of families, churches, schools, businesses, social groups, a state, and a nation, we must be vigilant and committed to insist that all these groups act in responsible ways as well.

Our society is becoming increasingly diverse and multicultured. One dimension of acting responsibly means learning to value this diversity—to work for a peaceful and productive unity in the midst of racial, ethnic, cultural, and religious differences.

Acting responsibly toward others thus requires that we have the ability to appreciate our own worth and importance. Appreciating our own worth is the foundation from which we are able to recognize and act in appreciation of the value of others. Informed compassion goes beyond sympathy. It actively values the differences in all human beings. Responsible caring for others means knowing when to say *no* as well as when to reach out. To act responsibly is to respect others as we respect ourselves.

In learning to appreciate our own gifts, we learn to appreciate and encourage the individual personhood and gifts of other persons.

And we become creative parts of a richer and healthier world.

No one can make us feel inferior without our permission.

—*Eleanor Roosevelt*

IV. Key Principles for Nurturing Self-esteem and Personal and Social Responsibility

*T*his section provides information on how we can establish, nurture, or restore healthy self-esteem, personal responsibility, and social responsibility. Acting against these principles is generally destructive to self-esteem and does not encourage people to take responsibility.

According to the definition developed by this Task Force, self-esteem is:

> **Appreciating my own worth and importance and having the character to be accountable for myself and to act responsibly toward others.**

Along with this definition, the principles outlined here rest on certain assumptions:

1. Self-esteem always develops in the context of social relationships. These relationships are internal (self-to-self), external (self-to-others and to the physical world), and transpersonal (self-to-God/cosmos/universe).
2. Each of these principles applies to every human relationship: self–self, parent–child, self–significant other, friend–friend, student–teacher, employee–employer, prison guard–inmate, psychotherapist–client, constituent–politician, consumer–retailer, and so on.
3. Nurturing healthy self-esteem relates directly to and provides a solid foundation for developing personal and social responsibility.
4. Being a responsible citizen depends on developing personal and social responsibility.
5. Being able to encourage or contribute to other people's self-esteem and their personal and social responsibility depends on our own level of growth in these areas.

Growth toward healthy self-esteem is always possible. All of us can change. Any person's self-respect can be restored. This document provides guidelines and suggestions for individuals, families, and community or educational groups who want to consider ways of fostering healthier self-regard within themselves and others.

These materials are designed to raise vital issues and stimulate thought, conversation, and further study. Toward this aim, a list of books follows the discussion of these principles. A more complete bibliography appears in the appendix of this report.

We encourage people to seek additional sources of information and assistance as they work toward raising self-worth. To acknowledge the need for other resources or consultants and then to take steps to find them are acts of healthy self-esteem and personal responsibility.

Acts is a significant word here. Increasing our self-esteem and accepting our responsibilities involve much more than reading inspiring words. We each need to translate the principles in this document into daily practice. In some cases, this is easy; in some, it is not. We can feel good about deciding to make responsible sustained efforts to grow and committing part of our energy to systematic study, thought, and action.

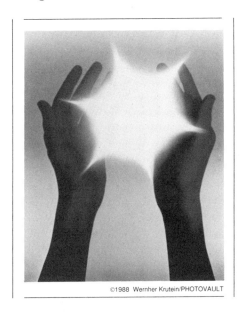

©1988 Wernher Krutein/PHOTOVAULT

Appreciating Our Worth and Importance

*T*he first category of key principles involves recognizing and appreciating our individual worth and importance. Several aspects of this are described in the following sections.

Accepting Ourselves

Each of us has a longing that cries out, "I want to be loved and accepted just the way I am." Sometimes we meet people who respond to us this way. Ultimately, we also need to learn to accept and treasure ourselves.

Accepting ourselves begins with an honest look at who we are. We don't need to like everything we find. We can just say, for example,

I own everything about me—my body . . . my feelings . . . my actions . . . I own all my triumphs and successes, all my failures and mistakes . . . I am me and I am okay.

—Virginia Satir, Family Therapist

"Oh, yes, I can recognize that I sometimes feel impatient. This is a human feeling, and I don't need to deny it or dislike myself for feeling it."

The point is not to become acceptable or worthy, but to acknowledge the worthiness that already exists. Our feelings are part of this, and accepting them builds our self-esteem: "I accept my feelings, and I accept myself." In turn, this lets us accept more responsibility in our lives: "I know I feel this way, and I can choose how to behave. I don't have to blame anybody else."

More and more over time, we can accept, appreciate, and celebrate ourselves as we are. We are each unique. We each can celebrate our special race, ethnicity, and culture. We can appreciate our bodies, our gender, and our sexuality. We can accept our ideas, feelings, and creativity.

Accepting ourselves does not discount the need for change and growth. Just the opposite: it is the first step we take when we want to change. We can decide to do something differently only after we accept who we are, where we are, and that we are capable of change. We can learn to swim only if we are willing to acknowledge that we do not already know how; we want to learn and we are capable of learning.

The curious paradox is that when I accept myself just as I am, then I can change.

—Carl Rogers, Psychologist

Setting Realistic Expectations

I have a dream that my four little children will one day live in a nation where they will not be judged by the color of their skin, but by the content of their character.

—Martin Luther King, Jr.

Once we decide to change, it helps to set expectations for ourselves. Our dreams and goals are like orchards: the more energy we put into them, the more they bear fruit. We need goals that are appropriate and attainable. Expecting too little of ourselves does not dignify our human spirit. On the other hand, unrealistically high expectations steal the beauty and joy from our achievements. Expecting too much of ourselves also damages our human spirit.

Some of us have uncommon goals. This is fine as long as they are also realistic. Marva Collins, for instance, has taught inner-city elementary schoolchildren in Chicago to learn Greek and Latin, do higher mathematics, and read the works of Shakespeare. She communicated her confidence that her students could do this, gave them information that excited them about learning, and encouraged them to take responsibility for succeeding.

Setting our own goals reflects our self-esteem: "I want to grow in my own direction, and I am capable of making competent and responsible progress as I learn." It is important to know that we are not on earth to live up to someone else's expectations. To make our unique contributions to the world, we each need to prize our individual worth and pursue our dreams.

Forgiving Ourselves and Others

To forgive means to stop resenting. When we let go of resentment toward ourselves and others, we are able to live constructively in the present. Forgiving releases us from the burden of hostility that eats away at our energy and self-esteem. Accepting forgiveness from others likewise allows us to move on with our lives.

New and difficult situations are more likely to become learning opportunities when we approach them with a nonjudgmental attitude: "This part of my work has given me trouble in the past. This time I am not aiming for perfection. I will do my best without worrying about how it compares with any ideal results."

When we permit mistakes, we allow ourselves and others to learn and to find more positive directions. Growth is possible when we are open to new ideas and possibilities.

Taking Risks

Developing the courage to explore new thoughts, behavior, and possibilities, to take appropriate risks, and to venture out across "safe boundaries" is necessary for learning and growth. A recent Carnegie Foundation study showed that the major predictor of sound mental health is people's willingness to risk.

Change is very frightening, even when it is a change we want. Often we feel more comfortable with a known problem than with taking steps in an unknown direction toward solving it. This is why some of us do not grow. We stay stuck with an old problem rather than risking the unfamiliar responsibilities of a new life.

For example, asking for attention without shame may be difficult because it is a new behavior. Taking the risk to ask for the attention we need is a crucial part of our growth. Attending to our needs encourages others to be responsible for theirs. Caring for ourselves makes us more capable of caring for others, and it encourages them to do the same.

©1980 Wernher Krutein/PHOTOVAULT

Trusting Ourselves and Others

> If you trust, you will be hurt, but if you don't trust, you will never learn to love.
>
> —*Mohandas Gandhi*

In the process of maturing, we increasingly come to trust the process of growth within ourselves. The psychologist Carl Rogers encouraged people to trust themselves enough to "feel their own feelings . . . and express themselves in their own unique ways."

Trusting ourselves, our judgment, and our competence inspires and educates others to trust themselves. Trusting others communicates that they are trustworthy. We cannot take responsibility for other persons' lives, and it is important to give them every opportunity to take responsibility for their own lives so they can learn to trust themselves.

We need to choose carefully when we trust. Trust is not an all-or-nothing proposition; we may trust someone with some things and not others, and we can build on whatever trust exists now. We can learn to evaluate the risks of extending a little more trust and, when warranted, we can take those risks. From our resulting experience, we can grow with our success or learn from our attempts.

> Few things help an individual more than to place responsibility upon him, and to let him know you trust him.
>
> —*Booker T. Washington*

©1987 Wernher Krutein/PHOTOVAULT

Expressing Our Feelings

> All feelings are honorable. The problem is how we use those feelings.
>
> —*Virginia Satir, Family Therapist*

By themselves, feelings are neither good nor bad. They are clues to our most crucial concerns, our deepest commitments, our needs, and our wants. We can learn to express our feelings in ways that do not hurt us or others. By expressing our authentic feelings, we also gain more awareness of our deeper selves.

Here is an exercise that may be helpful:

1. Turn your attention to how you are feeling. What part of your body feels what?
2. Recognize to yourself that this is how you are feeling, and give it a name. If you hear an inner criticism for feeling this way, just set it aside. Any feeling is acceptable.
3. Let yourself experience the sensations you are having. Separate these feelings from having to do anything about them.
4. Ask yourself whether you want to express your feelings now or at some other time. Do you want to take some other action now or later? Remind yourself that you have choices.

To become a whole person, we each need to grow in our capacity to express our true feelings immediately, authentically, and without manipulating others. For instance, we can say, "When I see you kicking the dog, I feel angry" rather than "You make me furious! If you had a heart, you wouldn't do that!"

Being open, telling the truth, and being authentic enrich our being in the world. We can share our positive feelings of love, caring, attraction, joy, relief, and excitement as well as sharing our anger, hurt, pain, sadness, grief, and fear. By honoring our true feelings, we can be in harmony with what we say, how we feel, and how we act.

Cultures differ in their ways of expressing feelings and respect. While honoring our distinct and varied traditions, we can learn from many recent studies about the importance of expressing affection. Especially with children (and also with adults), we can find healthy ways to nurture, to touch appropriately, to play or rough-house, to hug, and to show our love.

Appreciating Our Creativity

We are each potentially creative, and appreciating our creativity is crucial for healthy self-esteem. Creative expression takes many forms—from the artistry that appears in museums and concert halls to the artistry of raising children and building a business. In whatever form, creative expression enhances our experiences of individuality and personal power.

> Without creative personalities able to think and judge independently, the upward development of society is as unthinkable as the development of the individual personality without the nourishing soil of the community.
>
> —*Albert Einstein*

Appreciating Our Spiritual Being

Spirituality refers to experiencing ourselves in relationship to the universe. We refer to it in various ways: relating to God, to the God within, to our divinity, or to our higher consciousness. Being aware of our spiritual dimension helps us see ourselves as persons of value and worth.

> The ancients knew something which we seem to have forgotten. All means prove but a blunt instrument, if they have not behind them a living spirit.
>
> —*Albert Einstein*

©1978 Wernher Krutein/PHOTOVAULT

Experiencing our spiritual side is part of being human. Nourishing our spirit is necessary if we want healthy self-esteem. Meditation, prayer, deep relaxation, or other quiet times help us connect with our inner resources, our place in the world, and the sacredness of life.

Appreciating Our Minds

Whatever man touches is tinged with intentionality . . . Man's world is the world of meaning. It tolerates ambiguity, contradiction, madness, or confusion, but not lack of meaning.

—*Octavio Paz, Mexican Essayist*

Many times our pain and confusion arise from our habitual thought patterns. Over the years, negative images ("I'm too fat" or "I'm not good enough to do that") can come to dominate our sense of self. The longer we live with these thoughts, the more deeply embedded they become in our minds, and the more they seem like an accurate description of who we are. This seriously undermines our self-esteem and painfully distorts our behavior.

We need not remain captives of our destructive thoughts, however. When we are willing to look at our negative thoughts and images for what they are—mere ideas, not necessarily true at any moment—we can change our sense of ourselves.

When we replace destructive, inaccurate thoughts with those that are affirming, constructive, and honest, we become more joyful and productive people with healthier self-esteem.

Part of maturity is learning to discriminate between thoughts that build self-esteem and those that destroy it. Developing the will to act on thoughts and images that are healthy and responsible is an important part of the art of conscious living.

Appreciating Our Bodies

I believe in the flesh and the appetites. Seeing, hearing, feeling, are miracles and each part and tag of me is a miracle.

—*Walt Whitman*

Our bodies are simply and necessarily a part of who we are. To feel ashamed of our bodies or to refuse to accept them takes away from our wholeness as human beings, just as much as if we were to feel ashamed of our spirits or our minds. We may have learned this shame; we can also learn appreciation.

The respect and care we give our physical bodies reflect our gratitude for life. The body houses five senses, each of which serves a purpose. Making a conscious decision to understand, maintain, and develop the faculties of our bodies helps ensure our fulfillment. The more we enjoy using our physical senses and our bodies, the more we enjoy being ourselves.

By virtue of having a body, every human is a sexual being. Appreciating and affirming our bodies and our sexuality are essential to physical and mental health, self-esteem, and responsible behavior.

To understand the role our bodies play in bringing us fulfillment, we need to educate ourselves. Paying attention to the healthy development of our bodies strengthens our capacity to resist distress, illness, and addictions. Conscious or unconscious overindulgence of our senses can damage self-esteem and personal and social responsibility. A fuller appreciation of the unique nature and functioning of our physical bodies can reduce the pain and friction of life, leaving wonderment and joy in their place.

Appreciating the Worth and Importance of Others

Appreciating our own worth is similar in many ways to appreciating others, and both are important to self-esteem and responsibility.

He who is able to love himself is able to love others also; he who has learned to overcome self-contempt has overcome his contempt for others.

—*Paul Tillich, Theologian/Philosopher*

Affirming Each Person's Unique Worth

Whenever there is lost the consciousness that every man is an object of concern for us just because he is a man, civilization and morals are shaken, and the advance to fully developed inhumanity is only a question of time.

—*Albert Schweitzer*

Every human being deserves to be recognized and appreciated as a unique and valuable individual. To see and appreciate the contribution each of us makes to other people and the world, we need to acknowledge our unique strengths, positive qualities, and personality traits. Every one of us has unique gifts which are needed by the human community, and each of us matters.

We do not discover our true worth by comparing ourselves to other people. People do not have different worths. All of us have equal value as human beings. We can affirm all persons, their efforts, intentions, and worth. When we treat people in such special and positive ways, they look forward to their next chance to be with us.

Giving Personal Attention

The principal form that the work of love takes is attention. When we love another, we give him or her our attention. . . . By far the most common and important way in which we can exercise our attention is by listening.

—*M. Scott Peck, Psychiatrist*

All of us need to receive attention. To provide this for others, we need to learn to listen with undivided concentration and without interrupting. We also need to make people comfortable enough to ask us for attention.

We can do this by responding in ways that respect their dignity as well as our own. It is not enough to recognize this; we need to communicate our respect somehow—whether in words, gestures, or actions—and then make sure the other person understands our message of respect.

Demonstrating Respect, Acceptance, and Support

Human beings need to be treated with respect from the first moment of their lives. Our early experiences are especially crucial; they become the basis for deciding whether this is a world in which we feel safe, wanted, and valuable.

The importance of accepting and appreciating people as they are cannot be exaggerated. This includes accepting each person's feelings, thoughts, body, mind, and spirit. It also includes appreciating people's individual and cultural differences. We must make sure that we do not require others to deny or disown their real selves to earn our approval or love.

We live by encouragement and die without it—slowly, sadly, and angrily.

—*Celeste Holm, Actress*

Pacific Gas & Electric Co.

Accepting people does not always mean approving their actions. We can make this distinction clear in our thoughts, words, and deeds. Someone who tries and fails is not a failure, and someone who does something wrong is not a bad person. We can jail criminals or object to people's actions without condemning them as individuals.

Although we cannot take primary responsibility for other people's lives, we are responsible for creating and maintaining a society in which all of us are treated with dignity and respect. We can each find ways to demonstrate our respect and support for the old, the young, the different, and the disenfranchised.

Setting Realistic Expectations

Happiness lies in the joy of achievement and the thrill of creative effort.

—*Franklin D. Roosevelt*

It is important for us to encourage excellence in personal, academic, artistic, athletic, social, spiritual, and work skills. We can do this within families, schools, and other community groups. Living with expectations creates meaning and direction in people's lives. They gain a sense of self-confidence and personal satisfaction from discovering, developing, and expressing their abilities.

Our healthiest goals and strivings arise from an inborn and indestructible sense of personal worth. The reverse is not true, though: we harm children and adults when we equate their worth or loveability with their achievements. With this is mind, we need to make sure that any goals we propose for others are realistic, appropriate, and attainable.

Providing a Sensible Structure

Home is the place where boys and girls first learn how to limit their wishes, abide by rules, and consider the rights and needs of others.

—*Sidonie Gruenberg, Psychotherapist*

To explore and grow, human beings need a clear sense of structure. We need limits, guidance, and rules that are enforced consistently and fairly. These define an arena within which we feel secure enough to explore the world and ourselves. Knowing what our structure is lets us operate without fearing that our ventures will lead us into rejection, despair, or loss.

In our families, schools, and other institutions, we can help create clear rules and consequences that are understood by all the people involved. The point is to define our structure so we all feel free to move and learn.

Forgiving Others

To err is human, to forgive divine.
—Alexander Pope, English Writer

The more we can look honestly into ourselves, accepting and forgiving what we find there, the more we can accept and forgive other human beings. Hanging on to grudges or resentments limits our relationships and our ability to grow.

We develop our humanity by being more open, trusting, and affirming in our relationships with others. Attempting to control people by guilt or shame may achieve temporary goals, but it also creates enduring resentment and self-hatred.

Taking Risks

Learning . . . is not without risk; there is always more to be learned. But it is a glorious risk. The only time the risk becomes fierce and unacceptable is when one seeks to avert it.
—Norman Cousins, Writer

We help our children, friends, and associates when we encourage them to take risks that are necessary and appropriate for their growth and self-realization. We can do this by our words, attitudes, and example. The word *risk* recognizes that not all ventures succeed. Even such occasions, however, can be positive learning experiences. For the most part, we humans grow when we face the consequences of our behavior.

So, instead of protecting other people from the consequences of what they have done, we can be of more help by assisting them in correcting errors. We can alert them to what they have done; we may be able to show them an alternative they did not already know about, and they also benefit by being more likely to succeed in future attempts.

Mistakes are a natural part of life. We learn by experimenting; mistakes and failures can be important parts of our learning process. Einstein flunked grade-school mathematics. Edison tried over 9,000 kinds of filament before he found one that would work in a light bulb. Walt Disney went bankrupt five times before he built Disneyland. If we accept our setbacks, we can continue to risk, learn, and move on with excitement and satisfaction.

Appreciating the Benefits of a Multicultural Society

Diversity is a source of strength and balance. We add to our lives when we appreciate and accept the cultural and ethnic differences in our society. We also need to be aware that our rich cultural diversity is made possible by our commitment to be "one nation under God, with liberty and justice for all."

California is characterized by unprecedented ethnic, racial, and cultural diversity. We continue having the opportunity and challenge

How monotonous the sounds of the forest
would be if the music came only from
the top ten birds.

—*Unknown*

©1984 Wernher Krutein/PHOTOVAULT

to create a truly multicultural democracy. We benefit ourselves and
our society by growing in our self-esteem to the point where we are
able to welcome and feel comfortable with persons of all backgrounds.

Accepting Emotional Expressions

If we admit our depression openly and freely,
those around us get from it an experience of
freedom rather than the depression itself.

—*Rollo May, Psychologist*

As a result of cultural conditioning, many of us believe we should
never cry or be afraid. Some of us have been taught that we should
never be angry, aggressive, or confrontational. As a result, most of us
feel some shame when we honestly express our innermost feelings.

We need to accept, appreciate, and encourage each other's experiences and expressions of authentic feelings. We enhance each other's
self-esteem and health when we provide an environment in which
persons feel safe to experience themselves speaking and behaving in
ways that are consistent with their deepest selves. Such opportunities
allow them to discover and appreciate their own uniqueness, to be
more alive, and to share their richness with us.

Though our society regularly applauds the virtue of honesty, that
rarely extends to creating an atmosphere in which honest expressions
are in fact encouraged, accepted, and affirmed. It isn't easy for people
to express their feelings honestly if they suspect they will be ridiculed,
punished, or shunned for their statements. If we want honesty, we
must act to make it possible.

Negotiating Rather Than Being Abusive

Deeds of violence in our society are performed
largely by those trying . . . to demonstrate that
they, too, are significant . . . . Violence arises not
out of superfluity but out of powerlessness.

—*Rollo May, Psychologist*

Abuse—physical, emotional, and verbal—is always destructive. It is
never appropriate to inflict injury, shame, or humiliation on another
human being. To do so disrespects each person's humanity. If we
think of conflict as a problem to be solved rather than as a battle to be
won, we can negotiate with each other. Problem-solving communication can resolve the dispute and reconcile the people involved.
Everyone can gain and grow as a result. The more confident we are of
our own worth, the less we need to win victories over others to prove
ourselves. The more we recognize the preciousness of our own lives,
and the preciousness of all other human lives, the more likely we are
to find reasonable and respectful ways of dealing with our differences.

Affirming Accountability for Ourselves

*B*eyond appreciating our own worth and the worth of others, accepting responsibility for ourselves is the third category of key principles related to self-esteem, personal responsibility, and social responsibility.

Taking Responsibility for Our Own Decisions and Actions

One's philosophy is not best expressed in words. It is expressed in the choices one makes. . . . The process never ends until we die. And the choices we make are ultimately our responsibility.

—*Eleanor Roosevelt*

Throughout history humans have struggled between the risks of freedom and the temporary securities of slavery. That same choice confronts each of us today. As we take more responsibility for our choices and actions, we feel more joy as well as more freedom.

Our ability to weigh the issues in a problem, make a decision, and accept responsibility for that decision are important measures of maturity. Accepting responsibility means not blaming other people or circumstances if our choices prove to be painful or in error.

Another aspect of being responsible in our choices is our willingness to make commitments. In a society in which so many items are *disposable*, some of us treat commitments the same way. Yet it is only by committing ourselves to live through difficult and demanding times, without running away or seeking immediate relief, that we grow as persons and in our relationships.

Being a Person of Integrity

Integrity is the state of being complete and whole. When we have integrity, our thoughts, words, and actions are consistent with each other and reflect our professed philosophy and our deepest values.

—*Emmett Miller, Physician*

Living with integrity is essential to valuing ourselves. One important aspect of integrity is being honest in our dealings with other people, which requires being honest with ourselves. This does not mean using abrasive or destructive language or behavior ("brutal honesty"); instead, it means speaking our truth plainly and without blaming anyone for our feelings, thoughts, and actions.

In earliest childhood we develop self-protective justifications that enable us to avoid looking at ourselves openly. Gaining maturity is a process that includes taking that honest look at ourselves, acknowledging the excuses we use, and switching from those self-protective and restrictive blinders to more open and rewarding ways of being.

An honest, fully responsible, consciously directed life-style indicates healthy self-esteem. It also nurtures growth in self-esteem.

Understanding and Affirming Our Values

Growing and becoming our own unique selves require embracing and practicing some basic values. These can include but are not limited to trust, freedom, forgiveness, honesty, integrity, truth, patience, openness with ourselves and others, courtesy, responsibility, cooperation, due process, compassion, self-discipline, tolerance, sportsmanship, courage, reason, diversity, respect, civility, family nurturing, participation, industriousness, and love.

Affirming and nurturing values and healthy behaviors are essential for fostering positive and responsible character.

Attending to Our Physical Health

Physical activity helps improve our health and sense of well being. Exercising has many positive effects on our minds. If we cannot function normally in daily activities, on the other hand, our self-esteem may suffer.

Our vitality and ability to live well in the midst of stress depends on our physical and emotional health. Poor stress management contributes to problems such as heart disease, ulcers, mental breakdowns, and emotional collapse. Under stress, some people turn to stimulants or intoxicants; these rob us of essential nutrients and can damage the nervous system, making it difficult to achieve healthy bodies, minds, and self-esteem.

The best motivator for taking good care of our health is a deeply felt sense of our own worth. When we care for ourselves, we give our bodies respect, a balanced diet of nutritious foods, and adequate exercise.

Taking Responsibility for Our Actions as Parents

Recognizing the importance of their enormous task, responsible parents reach out for insights and information on creative and loving ways to raise their children. As we add to our understanding and skills as parents, we inevitably discover things we would do differently.

We are always growing and, therefore, always finding more constructive and healthier methods. When we make these discoveries, it is important not to waste time feeling guilty. Guilt only stifles our growth and detracts from our ability to function effectively as parents. Instead, we can acknowledge and accept our past, celebrate our new understanding, and take whatever steps we need to change.

We also need to respect and nurture our children's choice-making capacities and responsibilities. As parents, we can help them learn to take charge of their own lives, bit by bit, year by year. This requires understanding that they naturally make mistakes as they learn, that their brains are still developing, and that they can fully grasp certain concepts only at certain stages of their development.

Today's world includes a variety of parental situations. Whatever the particular family style, parents can benefit from recognizing their strengths and limitations. This allows them to reach out for information or assistance as they or their children need it.

In many ways, the respect and nurturing our children need from us are similar to what we all need from people in authority (our teachers, employers, police officers, politicians, and so on). Rather than being lecturers who mold our children into preset images of what we would like them to be, we can act as ladders to help them over the hurdles and obstacles they encounter as they make their own way through life.

Pacific Gas & Electric Co.

Affirming Our Responsibility Toward Others

*T*he fourth category of key principles has to do with acting responsibly toward each other.

Respecting the Dignity of Being Human

When people begin to ignore human dignity, it will not be long before they begin to ignore human rights.

—*G. K. Chesterton, English Writer*

It is important for us to recognize that our most valuable assets are within us. Our inner strengths, experiences, and truths cannot be lost, destroyed, or taken away. Every person has an inborn worth and can contribute to the human community. We can all treat each other with dignity and respect, provide opportunities to grow toward our fullest lives, and help each other discover and develop our unique gifts. We each deserve this, and we all can extend it to others.

Encouraging Independence, Autonomy, and Competence

We act responsibly when we encourage people to grow beyond dependence toward independence and interdependence. Counselors suggest, "Don't tie a child's shoe if she or he can do it. Encourage employees to figure out their own solutions to problems. Be a facilitator rather than a rescuer. Treat people as capable."

To give a man a loaf of bread is to feed him for a day. To teach him how to grow wheat is to feed him for a lifetime.

—Chinese Proverb

Do what you can, with what you have, where you are.

—Theodore Roosevelt

Young people need to struggle—and to succeed—to learn how to endure and to develop a sense of competence. We can support them and help them rise above negative comments (such as, "Who do you think you are?").

Some of us need assistance in standing up for ourselves and asking for what we need. To this end, we can help each other by learning assertiveness and negotiation skills. We can let people know that it's okay to ask for what they want, even if we may not be able to give it to them.

People need encouragement to *stretch*, to go for their dreams, to be confident of their decision-making capabilities, and to risk success.

Creating a Sense of Belonging

No man is an island, entire of itself; every man is a piece of the continent, a part of the main.

—John Donne, English Poet

All human beings want to belong. Belonging provides the foundation for our individual identity, freedom, and growth. We cannot esteem ourselves until we experience what it is like when others value and care for us.

Children in particular need a sense of belonging in—rather than being owned by—their families. Adults also thrive when they feel a part of a family. Ideally, our families let us openly acknowledge our experiences, including any weaknesses or mistakes, in a context of consistent acceptance, understanding, encouragement, and support.

One reason cults and teenage gangs are so attractive is that they provide a sense of belonging. Many families, schools, and communities do not offer this. Each community needs places where its citizens can speak from the heart and feel accepted. Support groups often offer this. Other possibilities include drop-in teen centers, with volunteers trained to listen and respond in caring ways.

Developing Basic Skills

Once a person's overall strengths have been identified and accepted, that individual can then take responsibility for his or her actions and gain a sense of direction, increased confidence, and improved feelings of self-esteem.

—Connie Palladino, Career Development Consultant

Basic skills are necessary to live in the world. Being able to read, write, add, and subtract, for example, are crucial to our participating effectively in society. We also need skills for employment; and as our world becomes more complex, we need more training to attain these skills.

Developing our skills leads to a sense of competence and self-esteem. Beyond our basic skills, we can also explore a wide variety of other talents: artistic, athletic, analytic, manual, and technological are only a few.

Our society benefits when we provide opportunities for all people to develop their basic skills. The more skilled our people are, the more productive and fulfilling our communities are for human growth and life.

Providing Physical Support and Safety

Self-esteem expresses itself in the tenderness and courage to stand up for others who are not able to stand up for themselves at the moment. Without encouraging dependence, those of us who have had the opportunity to develop our sensitive, expressive, and loving aspects are responsible for assisting others in their journey to more fulfilling and productive lives.

Our goal in providing others with support, physical safety, and assistance is to encourage self-esteem and autonomy. Persons who are injured physically, for instance, may need new tools and opportunities as they regain their sense of worth, ability, and productivity.

Fostering a Democratic Environment

When possible, we need to form our groups and organizations so that all members participate in establishing decisions, rules, and the consequences of breaking those rules. Family members, employees, students, and citizens who involve themselves in the decision-making process gain self-esteem and strengthen their sense of belonging.

Sometimes we feel that if we create democracy in the home, workplace, or school, we will undercut someone's authority and encourage irresponsibility. In fact, democracy works well only when we all exercise self-discipline and personal and social responsibility. Learning democracy at home creates the healthiest possible foundation for fostering it in our communities, states, and nations.

I know of no safe depository of the ultimate power of society but the people themselves; and if we think them not enlightened enough to exercise their control with a wholesome direction, the remedy is not to take it from them, but to inform their discretion by education.

—*Thomas Jefferson*

©1986 Wernher Krutein/PHOTOVAULT

Recognizing the Balance Between Freedom and Responsibility

Freedom without responsibility leads to destructive anarchy. Responsibility without freedom leads to slavery, to imprisonment of the human mind and spirit. An ideal society recognizes both freedom and responsibility as essential to personal and community life. By acknowledging the importance of each without emphasizing one to the exclusion of the other, we can keep a healthy balance between the two.

The aim of art, the aim of life can only be to increase the sum of freedom and responsibility to be found in every [person] and in the world.

—*Albert Camus, French Philosopher*

In the deepest sense possible, we human beings find our greatest freedom when we accept responsibility personally and thoughtfully. And it is in freedom, accepted personally and thoughtfully, that we find our greatest responsibilities.

Cooperating and Competing

Children who learn cooperatively—compared with those who learn competitively or independently—learn better, feel better about themselves, and get along better with each other.

—*Alfie Kohn, Author*

Research in the way children learn provides some important clues about dealing with each other in healthy and productive ways. Because we have so many models of competition—including U.S. history, business, and athletics—we also have a serious need to learn cooperative problem-solving and negotiation skills.

Overemphasizing competition artificially divides society into winners and losers. Cooperation and healthy competition, on the other hand, result in win-win situations.

Serving Humanity

The greatest good is what we do for one another.

—*Mother Theresa*

Serving the needs of our neighbors is part of our national heritage. With modern communication, we now live in a global village, in a way. We now learn about the needs of people all over the world.

Persons with healthy self-esteem choose to serve others out of their sense of personal fullness and their joy of being alive. In the process of serving, they deepen and reinforce their own self-esteem.

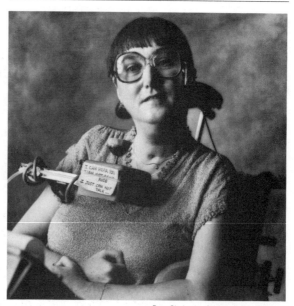

Dana Gluckstein—Courtesy of Apple Computer

Brief Bibliography on Self-esteem

*T*his brief bibliography is inserted here for the benefit of those who want to continue the exploration initiated by the foregoing "Principles."

General

Celebrate Yourself by Dorothy Corkville Briggs. Garden City, N.Y.: Doubleday & Co., 1977.

Feel the Fear and Do It Anyway by Susan Jeffers. San Diego: Harcourt Brace Jovanovich, 1987.

Healing the Shame that Binds You by John Bradshaw. Deerfield Beach, Fla.: Health Communications, Inc., 1988.

Honoring the Self (1988) and *How to Raise Your Self-Esteem* (1987) by Nathaniel Branden. New York: Bantam.

The New Peoplemaking by Virginia Satir. Palo Alto: Science & Behavior Books, 1988.

The Psychology of Self-Esteem by Nathaniel Branden. Los Angeles: Nash Publishing, 1969.

Release Your Brakes by James W. Newman. Costa Mesa, Calif.: H.D.L. Publishing, 1977.

The Social Importance of Self-Esteem, edited by Andrew M. Mecca, Neil J. Smelser, and John Vasconcellos. Berkeley: University of California Press, 1989.

What to Say When You Talk to Yourself by Shad Helmstetter. New York: Fawcett Crest, 1980.

Women

Bodylove: Learning to Like Our Looks—and Ourselves by Rita Freedman. New York: Harper and Row, 1988.

Women and Self-Esteem by Linda Sanford and Mary Ellen Donovan. Garden City, N.Y.: Anchor Doubleday, 1984.

Parents

Between Parent and Child by Haim Ginott. New York: Macmillan, 1968.

Parent Effectiveness Training by Thomas Gordon. New York: P. W. Wyden, 1970.

Raising Self-Reliant Children in a Self-Indulgent World by Stephen Glenn and Jane Nelson. Rocklin, CA: Prima Publishing & Communications, 1988.

Self-Esteem by Harris Clemes and Reynold Bean. New York: G.P. Putnam's Sons, 1987.

Self-Esteem: A Family Affair by Jean Illsley Clarke. New York: Harper and Row, 1978.

Your Child's Self-Esteem by Dorothy Corkville Briggs. Garden City, NY: Doubleday, 1970.

Education   *Esteem Builders* by Michele Borba.Rolling Hills Estates, CA: B.L.
Winch, 1989.

Inviting School Success: A Self-Concept Approach to Teaching and Learning
by William Purkey and John Novak. Belmont, CA: Wadsworth,
1984.

100 Ways to Enhance Self-Concept in the Classroom by Jack Canfield and
Harold Wells. Englewood Cliffs, NJ: Prentice-Hall, 1976.

For a comprehensive list of the numerous self-esteem curricula that
are currently available, write to the National Council for Self-Esteem,
c/o Gail Dusa, 6641 Leyland Park Drive, San Jose, CA 95120.

Business   *The One Minute Manager* by Kenneth Blanchard and Spencer Johnson.
Berkeley, CA: Berkeley Press, 1987.

Emmett E. Miller, M.D.

V. Further Action and Research Needed

*A*lmost unique among state task forces and commissions, the members of the California Task Force to Promote Self-esteem and Personal and Social Responsibility have chosen *not* to request an extension or continuation. The members feel their special function has been fulfilled. Some other structure is needed to continue this important work.

A committee of the Task Force has highlighted the functions which need to be continued:

- An on-going data base which continuously updates and evaluates information concerning current research and new programs in self-esteem and responsibility
- Continuing research and interdisciplinary studies in self-esteem, including but not limited to an academically accepted definition of self-esteem
- Workshops/conferences for students, teachers, business people, social service/government workers, and other interested groups
- A repository to house and make available the materials collected and produced by the Task Force
- Continuing coordination and support of the work of the various county task forces
- Assistance in implementing the Task Force's final recommendations

Just as this report was being completed, the Task Force received and liked a suggestion that would deal with the last of these targeted needs. The proposal was to request legislation that would provide for an "ombudsman" who would work with the Legislature and governmental agencies to facilitate and implement the recommendations and insights of the Task Force. As proposed, the "ombudsman" would be appointed by the Governor and confirmed by the Senate and the Assembly for a five-year term.

If such legislation is enacted, the "ombudsman" would effectively complement the other needed functions as they may be carried on by the county task forces, by one or more university-based research centers, and through projects undertaken by private sector organizations.

All of the University of California professors who did research on behalf of the Task Force agreed that more research is needed in each of the areas of their investigation. In addition, the enabling legislation

(Chapter 1065 of 1986 statutes—AB 3659, Vasconcellos) directed the Task Force to:

> *Identify and encourage further research and other available information relevant to the relation of self-esteem to the causes of the social problems enumerated herein.*

In the course of its public hearings, the Task Force received information concerning a number of additional areas of concern, problems that pose serious threats to the well being of individual citizens and to the society as a whole, and that are significantly related to the issue of self-esteem and personal and social responsibility.

The more prominent of these concerns that warrant further research and thought and action are:

1. *Aging:* In a society in which most indications of worth are dispensed on the basis of production and achievements, what happens to the self-esteem of those who are retired, who are no longer significantly involved in tangible production?

2. *AIDS:* The Task Force received testimony from people with AIDS and from those who represent organizations working with them. AIDS is the dominant emerging health issue at the close of this century, and more research needs to be done concerning its effect on the self-esteem of society as a whole, how the disease affects the self-esteem of those who are afflicted, how self-esteem relates to the ability of the afflicted to survive, and what can be considered proper and appropriate "personal and social responsibility" with regard to this crisis.

3. *Hunger and Homelessness:* Though this issue is touched on under the heading of "Poverty and Chronic Welfare Dependency," far more study needs to be directed to how a person's self-esteem is affected by hunger and homelessness and on the appropriate social responsibility on the rest of society to welfare recipients.

4. *Physical Disabilities:* On numerous occasions people with various forms of physical disability contacted the Task Force and made presentations at public hearings, asking that recognition be given to the struggles of the handicapped and disabled to assume a fully human role within our society.

5. *Racism:* The Task Force heard about the effect of racism on self-esteem during almost all of one public hearing and during portions of most of the rest. People testified concerning the effects of societal prejudice and also the different ways in which worth is measured within various ethnic groups. This is an area demanding further research.

VI. Recommendations and Discussion

*T*his section of our Task Force's report represents the substantive results of our legislatively mandated investigation into the relationship between self-esteem and the social concerns of: family (parenting, child abuse, and teenage pregnancy); education (schools and academic failure); substance use and abuse; crime and violence; poverty and chronic welfare dependency; and the workplace. Our data came from three primary sources: research prepared by professors from the University of California, public input and testimony from hearings, and the Task Force's survey of existing programs and state agencies. Each major area is organized in three parts: general findings, policy recommendations, and supporting data with program examples.

Given the complexity of the concept of self-esteem and its relationship to those social issues, it's hardly surprising that the Task Force eventually collected a virtual library of information. Reviewing and summarizing all these data and deriving practicable recommendations from the data took many months of labor and careful consideration.

From the beginning, we who served on the Task Force were determined that our findings and recommendations would be grounded in the most current and valid research available, including lay experience and anecdotal wisdom. Many of us on the Task Force are convinced that a sizeable number of practitioners in functioning programs are well ahead of academic researchers in their appreciation of self-esteem's central role in the social problems that plague our society.

Formal inquiry has nonetheless contributed significant insights. The research papers that several professors prepared for us were published by the University of California Press under the title *The Social Importance of Self-Esteem.* Neil Smelser, who edited the book, contends that the variable of self-esteem remains elusive because it is difficult to pinpoint scientifically. According to Dr. Smelser, this does not mean that the study of self-esteem be abandoned, but that the current scientific procedures be altered. (For a thorough discussion of the new research characteristics that Dr. Smelser recommends, refer to his introduction in *The Social Importance of Self-Esteem.*)

In the scientific literature, no consistently accepted definition exists for *self-esteem*, which makes it difficult to compare various studies. As a result, our researchers felt unable to establish *causal* relationships.

Most existing studies speak of significant correlations, which is customary within social science research. To paraphrase Martin Covington in his research review for the Task Force on academic success, just because the causality chain is incomplete with regard to self-esteem, it does not mean that it is implausible. In fact, the case for self-esteem is not only plausible, it is compelling. Current research findings essentially support the notion that improving self-esteem and self-esteeming social conditions can have a positive impact on many of our most pressing social problems. Professor Covington reminds us that the concept of self-esteem:

> . . . challenges us to be more fully human. In addition to being an object of scientific investigation and also an explanation for behavior, self-esteem is above all a metaphor, a symbol filled with excess meaning that can ignite visions of what we as a people might become. Perhaps it is only for the sake of self-esteem that we would be willing to carry out policy recommendations which seriously question . . . our most cherished beliefs.

For the most part, we have left it to individual readers, communities, institutions, and agencies to take responsibility for implementing these recommendations. Only occasionally did we address the Legislature or state agencies. The core process of change is one that must, finally, be the responsibility of the human community to make those changes necessary to create a California that is an esteemed and esteeming place.

©1986 Wernher Krutein/PHOTOVAULT

The programs cited in the text that follows are offered as effective examples of groups that are at work in these areas. Reliable authorities have presented them as being of good reputation with positive records of success. It is our hope that readers will find these listings useful for informational purposes. The Task Force is aware that many other programs of considerable merit exist throughout California. We sincerely wish we could have recognized each of them.

We of the Task Force are excited with the results of these three years of study, discussion, and decision. We believe that we have substantiated the premise on which this project was built—namely, that self-esteem is central to the personal and social concerns we face today. We are even more convinced that healthy self-esteem is central to positive possibilities for us as individuals, as communities, and as our state. We are grateful that so many Californians have chosen to share this dream with us.

The Family, Teenage Pregnancy, Child Abuse, and Self-esteem

*T*hrough all of our studies and research, we of the Task Force have become convinced that self-esteem is central to most of the personal and social problems that plague human life in today's world. And since each of us begins his or her life within a family, the conclusion is inescapable: the family must be the first and fundamental focus of our attention. As Virginia Satir said in *Peoplemaking*:

> *An infant coming into the world . . . must rely on the experiences he has with the people around him and the messages they give him about his worth as a person. For the first five or six years, the child's [self-esteem] is formed by the family almost exclusively. After he starts to school, other influences come into play, but the family remains important all through his adolescence. Outside forces tend to reinforce the feelings of worth or worthlessness that he has learned at home: the high-[self-esteem] child can weather many failures in school or among peers; the low-[self-esteem] child can experience many successes, yet feel a gnawing doubt about his own value.*

The family has always been the primary environment that shapes a person's values, perspectives, fears, dreams, and self-esteem. Only recently have professional counselors begun to be aware of the extent and subtlety by which those crucial influences are communicated. Even the most conscientious and well-intentioned parents are often unaware of the devastating effects of many long-accepted ways of raising children. Now we know that all parenting practices need to be examined and questioned. Without serious personal reflection, parents tend to repeat the same techniques that had such a destructive impact on their own lives as children. Another quote from Virginia Satir helps to bring these unintentional abuses into focus:

> *Every word, facial expression, gesture, or action on the part of the parent gives the child some message about his worth. It is sad that so many parents don't realize what messages they are sending. A mother may accept the bouquet clutched in her three-year-old's hand and say, "How pretty! Where did you get them?" but wear a worried, accusing expression that added, "Did you steal them from Mrs. Randall's garden?" In this case, she is building low [self-esteem] but probably does not realize it.*

Compliment what cannot be photographed.

—*Constance Dembrowsky, Founding President, National Council for Self-Esteem*

The Meaning of Family

With the radical changes in the structure of the family in today's society, it is all the more important for people to become aware of the critical influence of the family as the *welcoming party* that introduces each human being into the world. To encompass the range of currently possible family relationships — including nuclear, blended, single-parent, extended, gay, foster, and institutional families — the Task Force has adopted the following definition: A family is the set of two or more persons within which the individual receives his or her essential care and support. It is to this other person or group of persons that Virginia Satir addressed her direct statement of responsibility:

> *I am convinced that there are no genes to carry the feelings of worth. It is learned. And the family is where it is learned. You learned to feel high [self- esteem] or low [self-esteem] in the family your parents created. And your children are learning it in your family right now.*

The responsibilities of the family in preparing children for life in this world have always been demanding and difficult. Current changes in the family structure, along with the new threats from drugs and violence, bring the life-and-death significance of these family influences into even sharper focus.

Fifty percent of California's children will live in a single-parent household sometime before the age of eighteen. One in four California children are born to an unmarried mother. More than half of black children are born to single mothers. Almost half of all single mothers are at or below the poverty line (Kirst, et al., 1989). These families are often isolated, alienated, and lacking in community support, forced to raise their children in an informational and social vacuum that diminishes the self-esteem of everyone involved.

Only 8 percent of California's families have fathers who work full time and mothers who are employed at home. The number of mothers working outside the home continues to increase; it is currently around 50 percent nationally. Approximately 1.14 million children in Califor-

The high calling of parenthood must be more adequately recognized, respected and honored by our society. Therein lies the future of our nation.

—*National Council of Juvenile and Family Court Judges, 1989*

©1986 Wernher Krutein/PHOTOVAULT

nia spend time in some type of child care. Older children, for whom typical child care is inappropriate or too costly, often receive little parental supervision or nurturing guidance.

These changes in the family structure have powerful effects on the lives of California's children and represent a multitude of implications for their self-esteem and character development. This section focuses on the relationship between self-esteem and the family. More specifically, it addresses that critical relationship in terms of parenting, child abuse, and teenage pregnancy and parenthood.

Parenting and Self-esteem

Many times the Task Force has heard it said, in one form or another, "We are far better prepared to repair the engine of an automobile or cook a pot roast than to raise a child." This continues to be true in spite of reputable evidence of the importance of parental influence in child development. Stanley Coopersmith describes this dynamic between parental attitudes and behaviors and the formation of healthy self-esteem and personal and social responsibility:

> *The child apparently perceives and appreciates the attention and approval expressed by his mother (and father) and tends to view her as favoring and supportive. He also appears to interpret her interest and concern as an indication of his significance; basking in the signs of his personal importance, he comes to regard himself favorably. **This is success in its most personal expression—the concern, the attention, and the time of significant others.*** (Coopersmith, 1967)

Words of encouragement and approval do not alone constitute a healthy esteeming environment. Mr. Coopersmith's studies reveal that parents who foster healthy self-esteem in their children also have the following three characteristics:
- The parents themselves possess high levels of self-esteem.
- They consistently show respect for their children's rights and opinions.
- They clearly define limits on their children's behavior.

Recent family studies support the painful conclusion that parents unwittingly perpetuate destructive ways of raising children — sometimes because of ignorance, stress and frustration, and, more often, because of the experience of being reared by their own equally unprepared parents. It is clear that continuing disapproval, criticism, and punishment diminish the self-esteem of children. Children whose parents are unable to provide the requisites for healthy self-esteem, and who experience deprivation and injustice in their early formative years, often react by engaging in self-destructive and antisocial behavior, delinquency, and dropping out of school. In testimony presented to the Task Force, Thomas Gordon explained that such antisocial behavior can be thought of as ways that youngsters:

- Escape from or cope with what is painful, stressful, or anxiety-producing in their lives; and
- Satisfy important unmet needs, such as those for achievement, recognition, safety and security, acceptance, and close social relationships.

Effects of Child Abuse on Self-esteem

Statistics indicate that today's children suffer from an alarming rate of abuse at the hands of those upon whom they depend for nurturing and care. The most recent national data reveal that over two million cases of abuse are reported each year, including those related to physical, sexual, and emotional abuse and neglect. While reports have increased over 100 percent in the past decade, most experts agree that these indicate only the tip of the problem. At best, these reported cases represent only about 40 percent of the abuse that occurs.

Some researchers in this field are convinced that virtually all people experience unintended but actual emotional abuse at the hands of their well-meaning but ill-prepared parents, and that this is the source of a considerable amount of low self-esteem within the general population.

Besides the considerable physical and emotional damage it inflicts on its victims, child abuse destroys self-esteem and teaches violence as an acceptable means of handling frustration in personal relationships. The relationship between child abuse and low self-esteem is obvious to even the most casual observers, and practitioners in the field see that connection with frightening regularity. Kathy Baxter-Stern, Executive Director of the San Francisco Child Abuse Council, reports:

> *The Child Abuse Council has long been concerned about the low self-esteem many of our abused children show throughout their childhoods and into their adulthoods. . . . self-esteem, the core of our inner strength, gives us the ability to feel good about ourselves. Child abuse robs one of that ability at a very early age.*

Research shows that both the abuser and the child, regardless of the type of abuse, evidence low self-esteem. Abused children perceive themselves as having significantly fewer friends and are less ambitious regarding their occupational goals than nonabused children. Researchers have also found that members of abusive families experience depression and extreme feelings of guilt.

Abusing a child is often an effort to compensate for low self-esteem, a sense of worthlessness, by exercising power and control over the abused. In an effort to legitimize the maltreatment, the abuser pressures the victim into accepting low self-esteem and a distorted view of reality.

A loving environment in which there is consistent discipline is essential to healthy child development and the nurturing of positive self-esteem. Effective discipline is not synonymous, however, with physical punishment or harsh treatment that humiliates or degrades.

Parental warmth, defined limits, and respectful treatment lead to self-esteem in children.

—*Stanley Coopersmith*

In his classic 1967 study, Mr. Coopersmith examined the relationship between children's self-esteem, the effects it had on their lives, and the ways in which their parents fostered or hampered their self-esteem. He found that:

- Parents of children with low self-esteem were marked by a lack of affection, a need to dominate, little appreciation of good behavior, an inability to establish clear rules, and the use of severe forms of punishment.
- Parents of high self-esteem children tended to reinforce good behavior and did not rely on harsh disciplinary measures.

The parents whose children evidenced high self-esteem provided consistent discipline, held high expectations for their children's behavior, and were actively involved in and supportive of their children's activities.

Teenage Pregnancy and Parenthood

California has one of the highest teenage pregnancy rates in the nation: 143 per thousand for fifteen- to nineteen-year-olds. While California has experienced an overall decrease in teenage pregnancy since 1970, the same period has seen an increase in the pregnancy rates for those under fifteen years of age. In 1986 there were over 19,000 births to mothers aged seventeen years or younger in this state, and an estimated 357,000 teens were involved in parenting. These data suggest that many of those most likely to be bearing children are also those who are least prepared and least capable of caring for a child.

In the past, the majority of teenagers who became pregnant got married. In the last few decades, there has been a significant increase in the number of births to single teenagers. In addition, today's unmarried teens are less likely to relinquish their children for adoption than were adolescents in similar situations in the past.

While little research exists on the progress of these children, the available evidence indicates that teenage parenthood is often detrimental to the parents and their children. These mothers are more likely than those who are married to live under the stress of poverty, to use nonfamilial child care, and to suffer from a lack of social and psychological support. Teenage mothers typically drop out of school and, barely able to support themselves and their children, require public assistance for some period of time. Because of their youth, inexperience, and seemingly powerless situations, these mothers are at high risk to abuse their children.

Data indicate that many teenage fathers have histories of delinquency, substance abuse, failure to graduate from high school, financial difficulty, and exposure to family violence. This background makes it difficult for the teenage father to create a stable self-esteeming environment for his offspring.

A teenager may engage in sexual activity in an attempt to bolster low self-esteem. A female adolescent may expect motherhood to improve her status: as a mother, she is someone with an important task to perform, someone loved and needed. A boy may hope to enhance his self-worth by proving his sexual powers and virility. There is also evidence that a teenager with low self-esteem may be less concerned with pregnancy, feeling there is little to lose emotionally, educationally, or occupationally (Bhatti, et al., 1989).

One study reported that sexually active females had become sexually involved because they couldn't say no, because they wanted to satisfy a boyfriend, or because they felt it was expected of them — all reasons consistent with feelings of low self-esteem.

A number of well-designed longitudinal studies have correlated low self-esteem with infrequent use of contraceptives by females. (While most of these studies have focused on females, the Task Force wants to emphasize that the responsibility for pregnancy and its effects should be shared by both males and females.) High self-esteem females are more apt to rely on contraception to avoid pregnancy. Adolescents who choose not to use contraceptives and who later become teenage mothers are significantly more likely to have reported self-devaluing experiences and are less likely to perceive themselves as competent.

According to H. B. Kaplan, et al. (1979), youth with high self-esteem are those "who have positive experiences in their families and schools, feel good about themselves, and want to maintain the good will and respect of the people in these contexts. To do so, they behave in ways that will have this effect." Contrary to this, teenage mothers have been shown to devalue their experiences with family, school, and peers — conditions consistent with their registering the lowest self-esteem scores.

There is considerable evidence that high self-esteem in boys and girls promotes goals and attitudes that are incompatible with early pregnancy.

Parents need time to be involved in their children's daily lives, help them with their homework, know their friends, and answer their questions.

—*The California Joint Select Task Force on the Changing Family, 1989*

Summary to Family and Self-esteem

While subsequent learning and experience continue to shape the self and define its worth, the young child's primary lessons and experiences at home are the foundation from which all else derives. It is within the family that a child first learns who he or she is and what is expected of him or her. It is within the family that a young person forms the human bonds that to a large extent influence all subsequent relationships. Perhaps most important, it is within the influential folds of the family that a child does or does not feel loved, and the child's self-esteem develops.

Given the primary importance of the family in the development of self-esteem and of personal and social responsibility, we of the Task Force offer several recommendations that we discuss on the pages that follow. Our intention is to provide the family with the support it needs to nurture its children well.

Key Recommendations on the Family and Self-esteem

1. Develop a statewide media campaign to educate all Californians regarding the primary role of parents in the development of healthy self-esteem and personal and social responsibility; and provide appropriate, culturally sensitive multilingual training in loving and effective ways to raise children.

2. The Legislature should recognize the profound and primary role of parents by funding and directing the State Department of Education to implement culturally sensitive and age-appropriate parental courses for students throughout their educational experience.

Recommendations on the Family and Self-esteem in Brief Form

1. Highlight the important role of parents through a media campaign.
2. Include child rearing courses in the school curriculum.
3. Make courses on child rearing available to all.
4. Make self-esteem-enhancing child care available to all.
5. Provide health education for expectant mothers and fathers.
6. Provide self-esteem and responsibility training for all foster parents and institutional-care staff.
7. Reduce the number of teenage pregnancies through self-esteem training.
8. Provide family life programs for adolescents.
9. Provide programs to encourage responsibility of teenage fathers.
10. Provide support programs for parents at risk of abusing children.
11. Provide women's shelters that contain a self-esteem and responsiblity component.

Recommendations, Discussion, and Program Examples on the Family and Self-esteem

Highlight the important role of parents through a media campaign.

Develop a statewide media campaign to educate all Californians regarding the primary role of parents in the development of healthy self-esteem and of personal and social responsibility; and provide appropriate, culturally sensitive multilingual training in loving and effective ways to raise children.

Given the detrimental effect of harsh discipline on children, the practice of physical punishment deserves to be questioned. Parents, teachers, and child development workers need to learn more effective and less potentially damaging ways to discipline a child. Educators also need training to recognize children and parents at risk for abuse and those needing mental health counseling services, such as the ones listed below. Services like these deserve to be supported and made more widely available.

A broad-based educational campaign can be used to teach effective ways to rear children that rely on nonphysical modes of discipline. Such a campaign would also encourage families to seek help and reduce the stigma sometimes attached to receiving counseling.

Researchers believe high self-esteem may be an important factor in reducing teenage pregnancy, which again highlights the importance of the experiences children have at home and in school—experience that has much to do with nurturing a child's self-esteem. Ways must be found to allow positive experiences in family and at school, not just for the children but for all who are there. Rather than recreating what may already exist, the Task Force recommends analyzing and replicating current programs. Among those worthy of consideration, the Task Force found the following:

- **Early Childhood Center** (Cedar-Sinai Medical Center, 8700 Beverly Boulevard, Los Angeles, CA 90048-1869 [213] 855-5168): The Warm Line and PIPS (Preschool and Infant Parenting Service) offer guidance to parents to help prevent difficult or severe problems. Statistics for January, 1988, through March, 1989: 6,400 families were served on the Warm Line, 200 families participated in group counseling (per week), 600 individual family consultations were held, and 40 professionals volunteered.

- **Mother-Daughter Choice** (Girls Club of Santa Barbara, P.O. Box 236, Santa Barbara, CA 93102 [805] 963-4757): Funded by the Lily Endowment, this Santa Barbara program uses six discussion-group sessions in a home-based effort to stem the tide of teen pregnancy and drug use.

- **Parent Effectiveness Training** (Effectiveness Training, Inc., 531 Stevens Ave., Solana Beach, CA 92075-2093 [619] 481-8121): A program of training for parents, developed by Dr. Thomas Gordon, has received positive evaluations for more than 20 years.

RECOMMENDATION 2

Include child-rearing courses in the school curriculum.

The Legislature should recognize the profound and primary role of parents by funding, and directing the State Department of Education to implement, culturally sensitive and age-appropriate courses in parenting for students throughout their educational experience.

Numerous programs and curricula currently exist to teach people how to raise children. Virtually all of them indirectly or directly address the need to enhance children's self-esteem. Many such courses have been developed and pilot-tested by the State Department of Education. Others are private creations. Some involve training for students in general, some for prospective parents only; others involve the entire family. Child-rearing courses must be designed using content that is understandable and relevant to California's diverse population, including its various ethnic populations.

Education is one useful strategy, but being a good parent requires more than learning a set of skills. *Parents who create a nurturing environment are people who have healthy self-esteem.* It would be appropriate for the Department of Education to help schools to begin building self-esteem in kindergarten, while also offering support resources to the parents.

- **Nurturing Program for Teenage Parents and Their Families** (Family Development Resources, Inc., 219 East Madison St., Eau Claire, WI 54703 [715] 833-0904): Developed by nationally recognized Stephen J. Bavolek, Ph.D., and Juliana Dellinger-Bavolek, M.S.E., this home or school-based program enables teenage parents to learn infant and child massage, developmental milestones of growth, how to have fun with children, nurturing parenting routines, and ways to help children build their self-esteem and self-concept. Teens also learn about ways to delay pregnancy and handle peer pressure, sex, sexuality, date rape, personal power, and ways to build their own positive feelings of self.

RECOMMENDATION 3

Make courses on child rearing available to all.

Equip parents to fulfill their profound role by providing multilingual adult education courses in parenting at little or no cost throughout the state's educational and health and welfare systems, and as a part of community-based programs.

The most promising preventive approaches help parents develop insight into their own and their children's behavior, increase their social skills, raise their self-esteem, and enhance their personal relationships to meet their emotional needs. When this is done, the parents can be taught techniques that have positive effects on their children's general well-being, self-esteem, social competency, and self-efficacy.

Other community programs may be more accessible or appealing to certain groups than those offered by the state. Multigenerational school dropouts and their families, for instance, are not likely to be reached through efforts by the Department of Education or other educational systems. To maximize the use of resources and culturally appropriate outreach would require community collaboration.

It is not enough to provide children with self-esteem-enchancing programs outside the home. As Sherri Patterson, Project Director for Children Learning Assertion, Safety, and Social Skills project, admonishes: "If you want to have a self-esteem program for children, you must reach the parents. Without that, the parents may bequeath the legacy of abuse to their children."

The Task Force suggests that health insurance companies and hospitals be requested to consider funding such courses and reimbursing people's costs of participating. The Task Force also encourages the implementation of a promotional campaign to inform existing and expecting parents of the importance and availability of such courses.

- **Glendale Humanistic Psychological Center** (416 East Broadway Ave., Suite 115, Glendale, CA 91205 [818] 500-9835): This program provides sociodrama, psychodrama, and self-esteem courses for Hispanic parents and women. The parent education program focuses on the role of the parent, effective discipline, self-esteem, communication in the family, relationships, single and step parenting, and cross-cultural issues. The groups for women in Spanish are designed to enhance self-esteem, transform negative feelings into positive ones, and teach effective communication to improve human relationships.

RECOMMENDATION 4

Make self-esteem-enhancing child care available to all.

Encourage the availability for all children of adequate, effective, self-esteeming child care, which includes prenatal support and involvement, on both a continuing and a respite basis. Furthermore, request that existing licensing requirements be expanded to include training for child-care workers in the techniques for building self-esteem and personal and social responsibility.

Child care can be an opportunity for esteeming both children and their parents and for teaching parents about child development and child-rearing techniques that promote self-esteem. In addition, parents need to receive emotional support from child-care personnel.

RECOMMENDATION 5

Provide health education for expectant mothers and fathers.

Provide education for expectant parents concerning their responsibilities for the well-being of their unborn children, including the potential harm of poor nutrition, drug use, and the lack of prenatal medical care.

Recognizing their profound and primary importance in the development of healthy children who esteem themselves, potential parents need to receive proper information and guidance concerning their bodies and the effect their life-style would have on any child born to them. Their influence begins during pregnancy, so educating parents-to-be would also reduce the number of disabled children and allow for early identification of and intervention in prenatal problems.

RECOMMENDATION 6

Provide self-esteem and responsibility training for all foster parents and institutional care staff.

Make foster and institutional care available to all children in need, and ensure that all foster-care parents and institutional staff receive training in ways to enhance self-esteem and personal and social responsibility.

Training is available for foster parents and other out-of-home care providers through local community colleges, county social service departments, and in-service training from various private nonprofit associations. Emphasis needs to be given to the inclusion of self-esteem and responsibility materials in these curricula, as well as in those prepared for foster parents and foster youth.

For example, the Independent Living Program for foster youth stresses self-esteem in its training program, offering guidance in how to be self-assured and confident in handling the practical activities of everyday living.

- **Sacramento County Foster Parent Training Program** (7910 Betty Lou Drive, Sacramento, CA 95825 [916] 383-0751): This program provides training through a local commuity college for all licensed foster parents in Sacramento County. It is mandatory for all foster parents and is open to all social workers. The training sessions focus on the practical aspects of foster parenting, including guidance, discipline techniques, and self-esteem building.

RECOMMENDATION 7

Reduce the number of teenage pregnancies through self-esteem and age-appropriate sexual awareness education.

Encourage efforts to reduce teenage pregnancy rates through raising self-esteem, with the understanding that such programs provide information about both sexual abstinence and the availability of contraceptives.

The Task Force affirms the importance of self-esteem in a person's ability to be a part of nurturing, loving, and responsible relationships. Some in our day are finding abstinence to be a responsible expression of personal worth. Yet research in this area is compelling in its finding that merely enhancing a teenager's self-esteem is not likely to eliminate adolescent sexual experiences. Teenagers with high self-esteem who were sexually active and avoided pregnancy did so because they used contraception. Those with low self-esteem failed to use contraceptives for many reasons, and they became pregnant more often than those with high self-esteem.

An important aspect of anyone's self-esteem is an understanding and acceptance of his or her own physical body. How our bodies look, how they work, and how they are alike or different from others is a (right or wrong) way we have learned to measure our own self-worth. A positive attitude about our unique physical appearance, our sexuality, and the actual functioning of our bodies is often difficult to achieve and maintain. Children of all ages tell us they would like to know more about how their bodies work, and about the physical changes and feelings they experience as they develop through childhood and adolescence.

Over the years it has been difficult for parents, teachers, and communities to determine or agree on who should help our children learn about, accept, and understand their unique physical beings. When we ask children and adolescents where they have gotten the information and developed the attitudes they have, most of them say from their peers or the media. They also say they would have preferred to have been able to discuss these issues with their parents or other supportive adults. It appears to be our responsibility as adults to offer the children in our lives clearer and more supportive information, to provide guidance as they learn about and experience their physical selves.

The responsibility for avoiding pregnancy rests equally with male and female teenagers. All programs directed at reducing teenage pregnancy rates need to educate both males and females about the consequences of their actions, the reality and responsibility of parenthood, and mutual respect and caring in ideal relationships—as well as the skills needed to live up to their fullest potential. Such programs and courses need a specific self-esteem-building component integrated into the sex education curricula. Promising programs that have come to the attention of the Task Force are:

- **Adolescent Pregnancy Child Watch** (122 C Street, N.W., Ste. 400, Washington, DC 20001 [202] 628-8787): An offshoot of the Children's Defense Fund and in collaboration with the Association of Junior Leagues, the National Council of Negro Women, and the March of Dimes, this program trains and assists community groups in assessing community needs of local pregnancy problems and in developing local action campaigns and responses. The program also links the work of these projects with efforts at the national level and increases collaboration among different types of groups to bring diverse constituencies to work on adolescent pregnancy prevention.

I spent most of my years trying to control things, but I've come to realize that perfection is a self-defeating goal. I can now embrace life with all its imperfections, and it makes my days easier—a lot more fun. This is one of the most valuable lessons my love for my children has taught me.

—*Suzanna Matthew*

- **Adolescent Pregnancy Prevention Programs** (Hollenbeck Junior High School, 2510 E. Sixth St., Los Angeles, CA 90023 [213] 268-0176): Housed in Hollenbeck Junior High School, this program creates partnerships among school systems and community organizations to help prevent adolescent pregnancies.

- **San Diego Adolescent Pregnancy and Parenting Program** (2716 Marcy Ave., San Diego, CA 92113 [619] 525-7391): SANDAPP provides support services to teens. These include home visits, facilitating groups, and advocacy with community agencies. Self-esteem in teens has been enhanced by the individual attention and caring communicated by SANDAPP's case managers. Group activities have also enriched the teens through discussions, planning for and implementing activities, sharing the experience of being a teen parent, and solving problems through the use of a formal decision-making process.

- **Teen Outreach** (Association of Junior Leagues, 660 First Avenue, New York, NY 10016 [212] 683-1515): Created by the Association of Junior Leagues, this is a school-based program for adolescents that is designed to prevent early pregnancy and to encourage regular progression in school.

- **Young Parents Project** (10657 E. Bennett St., Grass Valley, CA 95945 [916] 272-2632): This adolescent family life program of the Nevada Union School District combines a diploma program with vocational guidance, counseling, and child care for teenage parents.

RECOMMENDATION 8

Provide family life programs for adolescents.

Provide funding for Adolescent Family Life Programs that provide qualified professionals to promote the self-esteem of teenagers while offering them and their families intensive management services. These programs need to be expanded into unserved areas.

The state budget appropriated $5 million in 1985 to demonstrate the effectiveness of replicating, on a statewide basis, ongoing teenage pregnancy and child-rearing courses. Accordingly, 32 Adolescent Family Life Programs (AFLP) received funding. Unfortunately, these programs serve only .01 percent of the potentially eligible clients. They also report 50 percent increases in the demand for services, waiting lists, and the need to prioritize those clients accepted according to greatest need and risk.

As AFLP projects developed and matured, the need for continuous, comprehensive case management services for adolescents became more apparent. The intensity and duration of case manager involvement increased while available staff hours decreased. As work with clients proceeds, more serious problems are uncovered, mirroring national trends: sexual and physical abuse, drug and alcohol abuse, prostitution, gangs, sexually transmitted diseases, runaways, homelessness, chronic illness, and welfare dependence. Effective case management requires ongoing, frequent contact to achieve client stability and self-sufficiency. The commitment to long-term case management fills most of the available time and, therefore, prohibits the enrollment of new clients.

- **Oakland Teen Parent Assistance Program** (Dorothy Patterson, Oakland Unified School District, 1025 Second Ave., P15, Oakland, CA 94606 [415] 836-8111): The stated goal of this program is "To meet the special needs of school age parents." The goal is accomplished by a competency based academic program, career and vocational exposure and training, work experience training, and support services. The support services include vertical integration of youth services in the community coupled with parenting skills classes and child care. This is a fully comprehensive approach to getting the teenage parents graduated, into jobs, and off to a good start as parents.

RECOMMENDATION 9

Provide programs to encourage responsibility of teenage fathers.

Within existing Adolescent Family Life Programs, develop pilot programs that will provide case management and family responsibility services to teenage fathers.

Teenage fathers need programs that educate and encourage them to participate, both personally and financially, in rearing their children. The heavy demand on AFLP services by teenage mothers makes this difficult. Nearly 60 percent of new clients enter AFLPs during their pregnancy. Without support to the father, however, overall program effectiveness is hindered, and projects are forced to ignore opportunities to intervene with males who will also face limited educational and vocational choices.

Increasing funds to programs such as AFLP would allow a broader community outreach to fathers than programs currently offered in the schools. While the public schools' K—12 classes can contribute significantly to primary prevention programs that teach boys to be responsible men, a third of the young fathers are beyond school age. A broader outreach and funding strategy needs to be considered to reach these fathers.

RECOMMENDATION 10

Provide support programs for parents at risk of abusing children.

Encourage growth in self-esteem among new parents by expanding, supporting, and making more accessible culturally and linguistically relevant programs that offer in-home child-rearing and respite services to new parents and those at risk of abusing their children.

The most consequential lessons about raising children are those taught, modeled, and experienced within the home. Because of their own history of being abused and because of stress, inexperience, lack of information, and low self-esteem, many parents are at risk of abusing their children. They find it difficult to seek help from the community. Therefore, the state has begun funding respite child care and parent-aide programs. These allow parents experiencing stress that might result in abuse to children to receive in-home help and relief, and the programs have been effective in preventing abuse. The mere existence of these approaches is a boon to self-esteem, according to Paul Crissey, Executive Director of the California Consortium of Child Abuse Councils, because they give parents the message that, "You are worth my time."

Emmett E. Miller, M.D.

These services need to contain a component that enhances self-esteem and personal and social responsibility for both staff and clients.

- **Children Institute** (711 South New Hampshire Ave., Los Angeles, CA 90005 [213] 385-5100): This family day care center provides English and Spanish out-patient therapeutic and educational services, with emphasis on self-esteem, child abuse prevention, and treatment through parenting classes and children's groups.

- **Hathaway Children's Services** (11500 Eldridge Avenue, Suite 204, Lake View Terrace, CA 91342 [818] 896-2255): This program offers outpatient individual, family, and group therapy on either a crisis or a long-term basis. The purpose is to enhance family functioning.

- **Stitch in Time Program** (La Cresta Foundation, 251 Panorama Drive, Bakersfield, CA [805] 323-0055): This nonprofit corporation offers a wide range of programs specifically designed to lend a hand at the earliest possible moment to stressed young families of children between birth and five years of age.

Support programs/groups and individual counseling are available to most abusive parents and their children on a first-come, first-served basis. In other words, while the number of programs available has increased over the past decade, the programs still fall short of meeting the demand at any given time. Often, even court-identified abusers and their victims face a waiting period before service can begin. Programs that are most likely to repair the psychological damage of abuse are those that address the needs and dynamics of the entire family.

- **Children's Self-Esteem Enhancement Program** (853 Manzanita Court, Chico, CA 95926 [916] 891-1731): Developed by the Family Service Association of Butte and Glenn counties, this program reaches out to children who are abused or neglected and works to enhance their self-esteem.

Provide women's shelters that contain a self-esteem and responsibility component.

Provide women's shelters that contain a self-esteem and responsibility component.

Spousal abuse encompasses a wide range—from psychological battering to murder. Research has found that spousal abuse often continues and escalates over time, usually becoming more frequent and severe. One study indicates that in 50 percent of domestic homicides, law enforcement had been previously summoned to the victim's home five or more times.

The domestic violence shelter movement was initiated in the mid-1970s by women to provide victims of battering with safe environments and counseling about their alternatives. The prevailing philosophy today remains to empower women through primary crisis intervention and long-term counseling. Shelter counseling programs are designed to help the survivor gain self-acceptance and confidence. This not only enables her to leave the battering situation but also to reestablish a new life for herself and her children. The children's programs teach children alternatives to violence (time out vs. hitting) and basic living skills (hygiene, safety, age-appropriate behavior, boundaries, etc.). Programs include esteem-building strategies for both the parent and the child through positive reinforcement, validation, and role modeling.

References for the Family and Self-esteem

Bhatti, Bonnie, David Derezotes, Seung-Ock Kim, and Harry Specht. "The Association Between Child Maltreatment and Self-Esteem," in *The Social Importance of Self-Esteem.* Berkeley, Calif.: The University of California Press, 1989.

Coopersmith, S. *The Antecedents of Self-Esteem.* San Francisco: Freeman, 1967.

Highlights of Official Child Abuse, Neglect, and Abuse Reporting in 1985. Denver: American Humane Association, 1987.

Kaplan, H. B., P. B. Smith, and A. D. Pokorny. "Psychosocial Antecedents of Unwed Motherhood Among Indigent Adolescents," *Journal of Youth and Adolescence,* Vol. 8 (1979), 181–207.

Kirst, Michael, et al. *Conditions of Children in California.* Berkeley, Calif.: Policy Analysis for California Education, University of California, Berkeley, 1989.

Miller, Alice. *Thou Shalt Not Be Aware.* New York: Farrar, Straus and Giroux, 1984.

Satir, Virginia. *Peoplemaking.* Palo Alto, Calif.: Science and Behavior Books, 1972.

Education, Academic Failure, and Self-esteem

Sarafin Zasneta of Southwestern College presented numerous studies to the Task Force that identify a correlation between a healthy self-concept and positive educational outcomes. In fact, self-concept is the most effective and consistent predictor of academic achievement, even better than test scores (Jones and Grieneeks, 1970).

Dr. Zasneta also testified that a student with a negative self-concept performs with the belief that he or she is incapable of learning. This condition leads to underachievement.

Failure to Learn

Failure to learn can be catastrophic for the individual and staggering in its costs to society. Many studies make the case that a significant number of our schools are failing at their most basic task, that of adequately educating our youth for a productive life. As Robert Reasoner, Superintendent of the Moreland School District in San Jose, testified to the Task Force:

- Twenty-five percent of all students who enter high school do not graduate.
- In some schools, 30 percent of our ethnic, inner-city students never complete the eighth grade.
- Among those who do graduate, 47 percent cannot write adequately.

The Committee for Economic Development, a group of national business leaders and educators, recently estimated that over a lifetime each year's group of high school dropouts costs the nation more than $240 billion in lost earnings and foregone taxes—and more still in expenditures for welfare and crime control (*Building the Future*, the 1988 Annual Report of the California State Department of Education).

Professor Martin Covington of the University of California, Berkeley, lamented that while these data are of themselves startling enough, "What is even more sobering is the larger implication of lives blighted, talent gone unused, and of minds wasted." (Covington, 1989)

School personnel and practices have a great deal of influence over the early psychological, social, and character development of our children. Schools can sometimes mitigate the detrimental effects of family dysfunction and abuse and even foster self-esteem where little previously existed. On the other hand, schools may—through insensi-

> ... parents and children evolve in tandem, supporting and challenging each other to develop ever more complete ways of knowing as they play out their lives together.
>
> —*Mary Field Belenky, et al.*

tive and overly competitive policies and interactions—undo the sense of worth instilled in a child by his or her parents. And while schools alone cannot be held culpable for the condition of our children, they should, working with parents and the community, be part of the solution.

Parents can create conditions at home that greatly enhance learning. Research indicates that reading to children, monitoring homework and the study environment, discussing school and everyday events, and taking children to parks, zoos, museums, libraries, and ball games can have a significant impact on success in school.

Self-esteem and Academic Failure

The Task Force investigated the possibility of a link between self-esteem and academic failure for the purpose of identifying the school and classroom conditions and teacher-student relations that might promote both self-esteem and academic success. Practitioners in the field believe that low self-esteem interferes with learning and suggests that high self-esteem may well promote it. Thus, school failures could be lessened by promoting those conditions known to enhance self-esteem and facilitate learning.

Martin Covington's research review for the Task Force asserts that:

> . . . at the heart of the achievement process we find a struggle which, when reduced to its essential elements, represents the need to establish and maintain feelings of worth and dignity.

Professor Covington and others find one of the culprits working against such sense of worth is the currently accepted practice of competition to motivate students. In a competitive system successes and failures become strongly associated with high or low ability. Ability is seen as an immutable factor, over which a failing student has little control. This promotes learned helplessness and hopelessness. That is, to avoid the feelings of worthlessness that stem from trying hard and failing, the student stops trying. He or she thus protects a fragile sense of worth by getting little education.

A number of schools are currently instituting methods that respect and nurture the potential all children possess to succeed. Cooperative learning or *team learning* is one of those methods. It is increasingly being applied to diminish the negative experiences sometimes brought on by large class sizes and too much classroom competition. Cooperative learning creates a network of peer support, encourages responsibility for self and others, and improves academic performance.

In testimony presented to the Task Force, Michele Borba reported that in the U.S. Department of Education's publication *Dealing with Dropouts*, young people cited as the major cause of their dropout behavior that "there was nobody there who cared." Dr. Borba also mentioned another study of 40,000 high school students in Arizona which concluded that making schools more effective must permit students to feel that "I am considered more than just a name on a roll

Pacific Gas & Electric Co.

sheet." Dr. Borba stressed the importance of enhancing a student's
environment. In her recent book, *Esteem Builders* (1989), she outlines
the "building blocks" necessary to help children gain a sense of
esteem and personal responsibility. They include:

Security—A feeling of strong assuredness wherein the child feels
comfortable and safe and knows there are people he or she can rely
on.

Selfhood—A feeling of strong self-knowledge wherein a child pos-
sesses an accurate and realistic sense of self in terms of attributes
and physical characteristics.

Affiliation—A feeling of belonging, acceptance, or relatedness that is
generally achieved in relationships with important others.

Mission—A feeling of influence and responsibility over the circumstances and one's own life, augmented by a sense of purpose and
aim that is self-motivated.

Competence—A feeling of successfulness in things regarded as personally important or valuable, combined with a general awareness
of strengths and an acceptance of weaknesses.

Preschool and Early Schooling

A child learns more during the first five years of life than during
any other five-year period. The basic skills, values, and perceptions of
self and others—acquired before a child enters kindergarten—form
the foundation of his or her future. The Task Force heard from early
childhood educators that they are increasingly in a position to affect
the well-being and self-esteem of our youngest children.

Whereas most children in the past spent their earliest years within
their own homes raised by relatives, many of today's children are in
some type of *outside* child-care situation.

Since a large number of mothers work outside the home, care must be taken to design programs supportive of and respectful to both working parents and their children. Some of this can be achieved by training early childhood educators to teach and manage children in ways that foster self-esteem and responsibility.

In addition, the Task Force was told of the need to keep preschool and early primary grades from becoming too structured. Moore and Moore, writing in the *Journal of School Health* (February, 1986), warn that early formal schooling may be "burning out" our children and teachers. According to a number of top learning and development authorities, including David Elkind of Boston and William Rohwer in Berkeley:

> *The learning tools of the average child who enrolls today between the ages of four and six or seven are neither tempered nor sharp enough for the structured academic tasks that increasingly are thrown at them. Worse still, we destroy positive sociability.*

The California Department of Education's report of the School Readiness Task Force, *Here They Come: Ready or Not!* recommended sweeping changes in methods of teaching children four through six years of age. Recommendations included a call for developmentally appropriate curricula and teaching practices; reduced class size; staff training; a change in assessment methods; improved links between public school programs and child care; parental involvement; elimination of work sheets and dittos; and an increased use of manipulative materials, such as blocks, paints, and objects to sort and count.

Summary to Education and Self-esteem

The building blocks of self-esteem are skills. The more skillful a person, the more likely that he or she will be able to cope in life situations. By fostering skills of personal and social responsibility, schools can help students increase their behavioral options. Having a number of behavioral options makes it easier to make ethical choices and develop skills to function effectively.

Education and the school experience greatly influence a child's psychological and social well-being, character, and productive potential as an adult. Accordingly, the Task Force makes several recommendations to help ensure a school environment that promotes self-esteem and personal and social responsibility for all of California's children and those who work with them.

Key Recommendations on Education and Self-esteem

1. Every school district in California should adopt the promotion of self-esteem and personal and social responsibility as a clearly stated goal, integrate self-esteem in its total curriculum, and inform all persons of its policies and operations.
   School boards should establish policies and procedures that value staff members and students and serve to foster mutual respect, esteem, and cooperation.

2. Course work in self-esteem should be required for credentials and as a part of ongoing in-service training for all educators.
   At least one course in the nature and development of self-esteem (in one's self and in one's students) should be required for credentials in teaching, counseling, or administration and for maintaining those credentials. School districts should develop and expand training in the development of self-esteem and personal and social responsibility as part of their ongoing staff development programs.

Recommendations on Education and Self-esteem in Brief Form

1. Self-esteem and responsibility must be woven into the total educational program.
2. Educate every educator—through pre-service and in-service training—in self-esteem and responsibility.
3. Give students opportunities to do community service.
4. Formulate a real-life skills curriculum.
5. Promote more parent involvement.
6. Be sensitive to the needs of students at risk of failure.
7. Use the arts to help develop self-esteem and responsibility.
8. Expand counseling and peer counseling services for students.
9. Provide cooperative learning opportunities.
10. Reduce class size or student: adult ratios.
11. Implement programs to counteract bigotry and prejudice.

Pacific Gas & Electric Co.

RECOMMENDATION 1

Self-esteem and responsibility must be woven into the total educational program.

Every school district and school in California should adopt the promotion of self-esteem and personal and social responsibility as a clearly stated goal, integrate self-esteem in their total curricula, and inform their publics of their policies and operations.

School boards should establish policies and procedures that value staff members and students and serve to foster mutual respect, esteem, and cooperation.

California schools are straining under the heavy burden of curricular change in every major content area as well as other major academic and social reforms. If self-esteem and personal and social responsibility become add-on topics in an already crowded schedule, their significance will be lost. If, however, issues and practical activities in self-esteem and responsibility were integrated in each curricular area, all staff development, and the whole environment of the school, people would be attending to both the ideas and their feelings at the same time without added classes.

According to the California State Department of Education, most of the schools selected annually as "Distinguished Schools" for their exemplary achievement and school atmosphere have programs to enhance the self-esteem of both their staffs and students. Further, research indicates a high correlation between how teachers feel about themselves and how students feel about themselves. Thus, structural and policy procedures affecting teachers are as important as the curricular changes suggested in this report.

In his testimony before the Task Force, Robert Reasoner, emphasized that a school's climate needs to encourage cooperative action rather than individual competition for rewards and recognition among teachers and staff. This recognition should include ceremonies and awards, opportunities for input, involvement in decision making, access to the decision makers, and the support required to enable teachers and staff to be effective.

Mr. Reasoner also encourages the use of team-building efforts to foster a cohesive climate in which each individual feels significant and supported by others on the staff. School goals must be derived through consensus rather than imposed by administrative edict.

Schools need to develop rules and disciplinary procedures in a collaborative manner among the administrators, teachers, parents, and students. Rules that are arbitrarily created and rigidly implemented, without input from those who must obey them, are likely to be resented and disobeyed. Rules and regulations must be clearly communicated so that students and staff fully understand what is expected. The intent of discipline is to foster self-respect rather than degrade it. Rewards for positive behavior and adherence to the rules should be as numerous as the consequences for misbehavior.

Model programs that have come to the Task Force's attention include:

- **Affective Skill Development for Adolescents** (5930 South 58th Street, Suite N, Lincoln, NE 68516 [402] 423-1623): This is a middle and high school program for enhancing self-esteem which includes training materials as well as student activities. The program has been especially effective with at-risk youth.

- **California Association of Student Councils** (313 West Winton Avenue, Hayward, CA 94544-1198 (415) 785-5583): This program provides training in leadership, conflict resolution, and communication skills for students and teachers.

- **Self-esteem Program:** (George Davila, 13174 E. Parlier, Parlier, CA 93648 [209] 646-3527): The Martinez Unified School District uses a self-esteem program comprised of a variety of materials, including those from the Center for Self-Esteem in Santa Cruz, California. The numerous components of the program include fostering self-esteem among teachers and students, presenting student drop-outs, and increasing attendance.

RECOMMENDATION 2

Educate every educator—through pre-service and in-service training—in self-esteem and responsibility.

Course work in self-esteem should be required for credentials and as a part of ongoing in-service training for all educators.

At least one course in the nature and development of self-esteem (in one's self and in one's students) should be required for credentials in teaching, counseling, or administration and for maintaining those credentials. School districts should develop and expand training in the development of self-esteem and personal and social responsibility as part of their ongoing staff development programs.

Provide training for day care and preschool teachers and staff in the techniques of self-esteem enhancement.

Currently, few universities and colleges in the state offer, nor do school districts require, course work in self-esteem. Learning about sensitivities and techniques of self-esteem enhancement should be recognized as an essential part of well-rounded training for all students, teachers, counselors, and administrators.

Courses in how self-esteem is nurtured and developed, how it is destroyed, and how it can be restored need to be made available to all staff—including administrators, teachers, counselors, aides, and noncertificated staff—as well as parents. All persons who, because of their professional or community positions, have an interest in themselves and in the well-being of children could benefit from a better understanding of how to enhance self-esteem.

A child learns about his or her self-worth and gains a sense of esteem, or does not, long before he or she enters kindergarten. Most experts believe a child's basic self-image is formed by age five. While it is never too late to enhance a person's esteem, the early years are especially crucial. Early childhood programs can teach children to feel pride in themselves and their achievements, to be independent and self-confident, and to begin to handle human relationships sensitively.

It is important that preschool and child care staff be provided training in the social, emotional, and creative aspects of healthy child development, as well as their skill levels.

Some of the staff development programs that were brought to the attention of the Task Force follow:

- **Action Education** (2831 Cedarwood Way, Carlsbad, CA 92008 [619] 434-6080): This program provides staff development workshops for teachers and administrators that promote affective and cognitive growth for K-12 students. Active learning strategies (cooperative learning, problem solving, communication skills) are demonstrated for each of the major content areas. The goal is to increase student self-esteem through academic achievement, personal responsibility, and collaborative effort.

- **Annual California Self-esteem Conference** (Bill Shuey, Center for Self-Esteem, P.O. Box 1532, Santa Cruz, CA 95061 [408] 426-6850): Cosponsored by the National Council for Self-Esteem, the Center for Self-Esteem, the State Department of Education, and several county offices of education, this is a yearly gathering of teachers, counselors, and school administrators who listen to top level speakers and participate in a wide variety of workshops.

- **Annual Southern California Self-esteem Conference** (the Foundation for Self-Esteem, 6035 Bristol Parkway, Culver City, CA 90230 [213] 568- 1505): Cosponsored by the National Council for Self-Esteem, the Foundation for Self-Esteem, the Continuing Education Institute, and seven county offices of education, this annual event provides expert speakers and workshops for teachers, counselors, and school administrators.

- **Los Angeles County Office of Education**, Office of Pupil Personnel and Guidance (Dr. Alice Healy-Sesno, 9300 E. Imperial Highway, Downey, CA 90242 [213] 922-6333): Sponsors an annual one-day conference for school guidance counselors, which always has numerous presenters on self-esteem.

- **Masters of Arts in Person-Centered Education** (United States International University, 10455 Pomerado Road, San Diego, CA

92131 [619] 693-4595): This program focuses on self-esteem in the classroom; its participants must be classroom teachers. It examines both practical and theoretical issues and has made an impact on the self-esteem of teachers and students for 15 years.

- **Santa Clara County Office of Education** (Educational Development Center, Charlotte Powers, 100 Skyport Dr., #237, San Jose, CA 95115 [408] 453-6624): This agency has offered a series of trainings in self-esteem over the past three years, reaching thousands of teachers in a five-county area.

RECOMMENDATION 3

Give students opportunities to do community service.

Time should be devoted to a study of the ways in which individuals can become participatory citizens through voting, jury service, volunteerism, and involvement in community organizations.

—*History–Social Science Framework California State Department of Education*

Offer opportunities for students of all ages to do community service work.

By the time students graduate from high school they should be well-versed in reading, writing, math, science—and responsibility. Growing numbers of voluntary and mandatory programs are springing up around the country to provide opportunities for youth to do community service. Educators report that most students who are involved in helping others become less selfish and more confident about their own abilities. The confidence carries over into their classroom work (*New York Times*, November 30, 1988).

Community service has the potential to provide desperately needed help for neighborhoods, cities, forests, and farmlands. And just as important, it can kindle civic responsibility, altruism, and self-sacrifice in a generation of young people that seem sorely lacking in those traits.

Administrators of the student community service program at the University of California, Davis say that community service encourages a long-term commitment to the community and fosters responsible citizenship and leadership on the part of students.

For many students, community service can also facilitate career development by providing an opportunity to gain preprofessional experience while building creativity and self-confidence. Many participating students have testified that community service enriched their high school and university experiences.

The following community service programs were brought to the Task Force's attention:

- **California Campus Compact** (Chuck Supple, Executive Director, UCLA [213] 206-3346): This program is part of a national effort called Campus Compact sponsored by the Education Commission of the States, headquartered in Rhode Island ([401] 863-1119). It is a coalition of more than 40 California colleges and universities, public and private, that help students help others, and it is cochaired by Chancellor Charles Young of UCLA and President Donald Kennedy of Stanford University.

- **California Conservation Corps** (1530 Capitol Ave., Sacramento, CA 95814 [916] 445-6819 or, to join, call toll-free [800] 952-JOBS): The CCC is a work ethic program for young people aged eighteen to twenty-three with a dual mission: the employment and development of young people and the conservation and enhancement of the state's natural resources. To carry out this mission, the CCC has established 18 residential centers throughout the state, as well as 30 nonresidential satellite locations and a training academy. "No matter what your future plans are, the CCC is an opportunity to increase your self-confidence, motivation, and direction."

- **Constitutional Rights Foundation** (601 South Kingsley Dr., Los Angeles, CA 90005 [213] 487-5590): With funding from individuals, corporations, and foundations, this program has offered law-related and citizenship education programs for 25 years. Programs include Youth Community Service, Youth Leadership for Action, Business Issues in the Classroom, Mock Trials, Law Day, and Sports and the Law.

- **Student Internships for Work with High School Students** (Dr. Stephanie McGraw, 400 Golden Shore Blvd., Ste. 318, Long Beach, CA 90802 [213] 590-5547): California State University students serve as mentors and role models in high schools with Hispanic and black enrollments of 60 percent or higher.

- **UC Davis Human Corps: Students Making a Degree of Difference** (Internship and Career Center, 2nd Floor, South Hall, Davis, CA 95616 [916] 752-2855): At the University of California, Davis, many students work actively with community agencies, including health care facilities, schools, private nonprofit organizations, and others. Student volunteers have participated in such projects as teaching migrant families basic first aid and working with the library literacy project.

RECOMMENDATION 4

Formulate a real-life skills curriculum.

The State Department of Education, in cooperation with the state's business leaders, is urged to develop an effective living-skills curriculum for every student in kindergarten through grade twelve, including self-esteem and personal responsibility components.

The Task Force believes that every California student needs comprehensive, structured, well-sequenced instruction in basic living skills, such as developing and maintaining good character, positive self-esteem, conflict resolution, effective communication, goal setting and goal achievement, time and money management, creative problem solving, leadership, stress management, and decision making; as well as in basic American values, such as responsibility, honesty, integrity, self-discipline, equity, and cooperation.

Many current programs and courses focus on various personal and career skills; however, there is no comprehensive plan for developing self-esteem or personal and social responsibility in the schools of California. Many existing programs are fragmented, too brief, and not integrated with the regular program.

Career development should be an important component of this curriculum. A career/life development curriculum provides motivation, tools, and information for identifying individual strengths and abilities. It also gives students useful knowledge about themselves, their career potential, and their personal and social responsibilities.

Assessment tools, hands-on experience, role models, mentoring, internships, and career day conferences need to be integrated into the course. Business communities and parents need to take an active role if our students are going to be sufficiently prepared for tomorrow. Once students have a clearer understanding of who they are and where they are going, they increase their responsible behavior and their feelings of self-esteem.

The State Department of Education should convene a broadly representative group to develop this curriculum. Included in the group should be university professors, curriculum development specialists, local high school district personnel, community and business leaders, students, and parents.

Some of the programs in real-life skills that were identified for the Task Force follow:

- **Aerospace Technology Magnet** (Gayle Quinn, Coordinator, 4400 Briercrest Ave., Lakewood, CA 90713 [213] 436-9931, ext. 1337 or 7124): The Long Beach Unified School District was chosen by the United States Department of Education for a major federal grant to open this national model of cooperation between industry and education. The program for minority students, grades four to eight, opened in six LBUSD schools in the fall of 1989. The students learn computer technology, aerospace science and mathematics, technical skills, and even take pre-engineering classes that lead to higher education. NASA, Jet Propulsion Laboratory, McDonnell Douglas, Northrop, and Rockwell train the teachers; and McDonnell Douglas offers work experience to the students.

- **College Readiness Program** (Ron Temple, State Department of Education, Office of Special Programs, 560 J Street, Ste. 570, Sacramento, CA 95814 [916] 324-7146): This program links California State University campuses with junior high schools in their respective areas to help sixth, seventh, and eighth graders achieve competence and prepare for college.

- **Partnership Academy Program** (Sequoia School District, 480 James Avenue, Redwood City, CA 94062-1098 [415] 369-1411, ext. 327): This state-funded program for the potential dropout student is operating in over 30 sites. The program requires the joint participation of business, government, labor, the community, and education organizations. A school-within-a-school concept, students spend three years learning a specific skill in computers or electronics. Supported by a team of English, math, and science teachers, students can also use their skills in industry-sponsored work settings that encourage career development.

- **Redwood Program** (Redwood City High School, 1968 Old County Road, Redwood City, CA 94063 [415] 369-1411, ext. 334): This is a continuation, half-day public school program for potential dropout students. Its focus is on the needs of the students, not rules and regulations. The program currently includes 180 students, sixteen to eighteen years old, and focuses on career/life planning. Short- and long-term personal, educational, and work goals are discussed. This is followed by written goal-setting strategies, career testing to assess specific strengths, and follow-up counseling to meet individual needs. Close contact with supportive teachers and staff allows students to feel loved and supported, and it encourages them to believe in themselves. The School-Aged Mothers Program enables girls to continue education along with career guidance. The Therapeutic Day School Program cares for those with special education needs.

RECOMMENDATION 5

Promote more parent involvement.

Parents need to become involved in their children's education; teachers and principals need to include parents in their ongoing plans, programs, and communications.

Educational research resoundingly concludes that what parents do at home with their children is a key factor in student achievement. For example, Herbert J. Walberg, Research Professor of Education at the University of Illinois, notes that the way in which parents interact with their children at home is twice as predictive of those children's success in school than is their family's social or economic status (Walberg, 1984).

Research done by Reginald Clark, Professor of Education at Claremont College, reinforces the idea that parents need to help their children with their education throughout their lives (Clark, 1983). Professor Clark's research over the last ten years refutes the idea that as children get older, they need less parental involvement in their education. He also found that the way in which schools communicate with parents makes a big difference regarding how involved parents become with their children's education.

Schools should foster family-school partnerships to engage the support and involvement of parents in their children's education. Such a partnership needs to enlist parental input in school programs, procedures, and curriculum development and to assist teachers in the classroom. Just as important, it can help parents learn skills necessary to improve their children's academic achievement and sense of self-esteem and responsibility.

A study by Brookover (1978) reported that using trained educators to help parents learn these specific skills increased their children's academic self-concept and achievement. In addition, a nationwide survey of 22,000 teachers compiled by the Carnegie Foundation for the Advancement of Teaching (January, 1989) reported that 90 percent of the teachers polled felt that a lack of parental support was a problem in their schools.

Routine interaction between school personnel and parents helps foster a shared sense of purpose and pride. Effective strategies need to

Pacific Gas & Electric Co.

be taught to teachers so that parent-teacher interactions are worthwhile for all involved. Parents need to receive information on the status of their child's academic, social, and emotional growth. And parents should be encouraged to communicate their concerns and knowledge to a

receptive school staff. A parent-school partnership needs to allow and encourage participation on the part of working parents as well as homemakers, fathers as well as mothers, and step-parents and other caretakers.

Nearly 20 years ago, James P. Comer, a child psychiatrist at Yale University, started the School Development Program (SDP) in two New Haven inner-city elementary schools—schools with the city's worst records for truancy, disciplinary problems, academic failure, and staff turnover (Comer, 1986). Central to this program is the belief that school and family must bond as allies to foster the children's development; to teach common, positive values; to enhance the children's self-esteem; and to prepare them—emotionally, morally, linguistically, and cognitively—for success in the "mainstream."

The SDP fostered collaborative teams composed of parents and staff. These teams worked together to develop curricula and social-skills training for students, hired parents as classroom assistants, sponsored social activities, and provided counseling for emotional problems. By the twelfth year of the program, the two schools had gone from last place to third in the city for academic achievement, and first in attendance. Since then, the SDP model has been successfully applied in at least 50 schools throughout the nation.

The following parent involvement projects were identified for the Task Force as exemplary:

- **New Parents as Teachers Project** (Missouri State Department of Elementary and Secondary Education, P. O. Box 480, Jefferson City, MO 65102 [314] 751-3078): Funded by the Danforth Foundation, this project is based on two premises: (1) that you are likely to make the greatest difference in the academic prospects of young children if you reach them during the first three years; and (2) that the most inexpensive and efficient method is to work through the people who have the greatest influence on children's lives during this period—their parents.

- **A Parent University Day** (Pat Lamson, Cupertino Union School District, 10301 Vista Drive, Cupertino, CA 95014 [408] 252-3000, ext. 611): Mentor teachers and local professionals offer a wide range of parenting courses on this once-a-year day. Local Girl Scouts offer free baby-sitting facilities on campus, and local businesses donate money for a noted keynote speaker.

- **Project Self-Esteem** (P. O. Box 480, Newport Beach, CA 92659 [714] 756-2226): This is a privately developed organization in Orange County that ties the parent-school partnership together with self-esteem enhancement.

- **Quality Education Project** (QEP, 2111 Turk Street, San Francisco, CA 94115 [415] 921-8673): This program gets parents actively involved in supporting their children's education by training school administrators and teachers in generating at-home support. This effort reinforces classroom instruction by training parents in ways to support reading as a family activity and by involving the business, medical, and religious communities in support of local schools.

- **Parent Involvement Unit** (State Department of Education, 721 Capitol Mall, Sacramento, CA 95814-4785 [916] 323-0548): This unit provides information on parent involvement programs operating throughout the state. It also sponsors staff development workshops and publishes a listing of successful parent involvement programs.

RECOMMENDATION 6

Be sensitive to the needs of students at risk of failure.

Encourage school districts to identify promptly those students with impediments to learning and at risk of failure.

*Support and expand programs to enhance the self-esteem, character development, and academic success of **all** students, with special emphasis on those in greatest jeopardy of academic failure.*

In her presentation to the Task Force, Michele Borba quoted the National Dropout Defense Fund report, which indicated that each year almost a million students leave school primarily to escape failure. National statistics highlight the high price society has to pay for the dropout problem. For example, only two years after leaving school, dropouts are:

- More than three times as likely as graduates to be unemployed.
- More than four times as likely to have been in trouble with the law.
- If female, more than nine times as likely as graduates to be on welfare.
- If female, married or not, six times as likely as graduates to have given birth.

Early identification of any difficulty that interferes with the learning process can result in effective steps to enhance a student's self-esteem and school performance.

Caution must be exercised, however, to ensure that low expectations and negative self-fulling prophecies are not fostered by early identification. Numerous studies attest to the important relationship between teacher expectations and student self-esteem and academic achievement. Teachers need to recognize the enormous power they have over their students' self-perceptions and to take great care not to stigmatize or segregate students who require special assistance. Teachers need to receive training in the variety of learning styles and types of intelligence evidenced by students.

According to Robert Reasoner, successful programs in dealing with this issue are designed to develop specific attitudes, understanding, and skills that enhance self-esteem, including self-understanding, communication skills, social skills, and decision-making and goal-setting skills. The various approaches taken fall into four categories:

- **The cognitive approach** helps children evaluate the negative attitudes and emotions they hold that may be barriers to their personal progress. (The basic premise is that negative emotions stem *not* from events themselves but from a system of internal beliefs and ideas about those events.) Course materials help children replace unreasonable and irrational thinking with more realistic and rational ways of dealing more effectively with situations.

- **The behavioral approach** focuses on changing the behavior students exhibit. When children with a lack of self-esteem learn to use behavior that commands respect, those children feel better about themselves, and others relate to them differently.

- **The experiential approach** plans and conducts specific experiences for children that allow them to have positive feelings and receive affirmations from others. This is perhaps the most common approach, and elements of this technique can be found in most programs.

- **The environmental approach** structures the learning environment so that students develop specific skills and experience attitudes that contribute to self-esteem. Given conditions that foster security, self-acceptance, belongingness or connectedness, purpose, and efficiency, children begin to function more effectively and capitalize on their own inner sources for self-esteem.

Current programs that claim to promote self-esteem need to be evaluated for effectiveness. Those found to be exemplary should be replicated where possible and analyzed to determine the common aspects that seem to account for their successes. Key components of these programs, such as the ones cited below, could be used as standards and guidelines for developing future programs.

- **The Achievement Council** (In Oakland: Dr. Susana Naverro [415] 839-4647, and in Los Angeles: Dr. Ruth Johnson [213] 487-3194): Since its inception in 1985, the Achievement Council has worked intensively with administration and faculties in over 100 predominantly minority schools through a variety of initiatives designed to raise student achievement. It has no funds to offer but provides the schools with access to the expertise and resources they need. Staff on several University of California and California State University campuses work with schools through these programs.

- **Building Self-Esteem Program** (Center for Self-Esteem, P.O. Box 1532, Santa Cruz, CA 95060 [408] 426-6850): This program includes material for administrators, teachers, and parents, based on a framework substantiated by research. The framework is built around the development of five basic attitudes: a sense of security, identity, belonging, purpose, and personal competence. The material is designed for kindergarten through grade eight. A section for secondary schools is due in 1990.

- **Choices and Challenges** (Advocacy Press, P.O. Box 236, Department SI, Santa Barbara, CA 93102 [805] 962-2728): This is a program designed to help adolescents build self-awareness, practice goal setting, clarify values, improve decision making, and research career options.

- **Culver City Self-Esteem Model School Project** (Dr. Vera Jashni, Culver City Unified School District, 4034 Irving Place, Culver City, CA 90232 [213] 839-4361, ext. 213): This project implements the curriculum guide *Self-Esteem in the Classroom*, which contains over 250 activities to build high self-esteem, based on the notion that students attain positive self-concepts by becoming actively involved with the effective functioning of their bodies, minds, and emotions. Skills include positive thinking, accepting feelings, communication skills, support groups, and goal setting.

- **The Dynamics of Relationships** (Equal Partners, 11348 Connecticut Ave., Kensington, MD 20895 [301] 933-1489): This is a semester course for adolescents, with information on self-esteem, communication, gender roles, affection, expectations, dating, marriage, and parenthood.

- **The Foundation for Self-Esteem** (6035 Bristol Parkway, Culver City, CA 90230 [213] 568-1505): This privately funded foundation has developed training materials (K-16) to develop self-esteem and academic achievement.

- **It's Funner to Be a Runner** (Peter P. Saccone, 2427 Nielsen St., El Cajon, CA 92020 [619] 258-9694): Developed in the Cajon Valley Union School District for elementary school students, this program combines physical fitness with learning and self-esteem skills.

- **How to Be Successful in Less Than Ten Minutes a Day** (Thomas Jefferson Center, 202 S. Lake, Ste. 240, Pasadena, CA 91101 [818] 792-8130): This ten-minute daily homeroom program, taught by all teachers, fosters personal and social responsibility skills and self-esteem- building activities. The skills include being on time, being prepared, and being a good listener. The activities include goal setting, planning for the future, and characteristics of successful people. The program also offers a progress handbook to help the staff and student body focus on personal responsibility skills.

- **"Pumsy: In Search of Excellence"** and **"Thinking, Changing, and Rearranging"** by Jill Anderson (Timberline Press, P.O Box 70071, Eugene, OR 97401 [503] 345-1771): Course materials help children replace unreasonable thinking with more rational thoughts.

- **Responsibility Skills—Lessons for Success** (Thomas Jefferson Center, 202 S. Lake, Ste. 240, Pasadena, CA 91101 [818] 792-8130): Written by teachers for teachers, this K—6 curriculum provides model lessons to teach students to be responsible. Introduced in each class for 15 to 20 minutes every Monday, the lessons are then infused into the general curriculum throughout the remainder of the week. Skills include how to be a goal setter, how to be a risk taker, how to be polite, how to be on time, and how to be confident.

- **Teacher Expectations and Student Achievement** (Elsa Brizzi, TESA Program Director, Los Angeles County Education Center, 9300 Imperial Highway, Downey, CA 90242-2890 [213] 922-6167): An in-service training program for teachers of all subjects (K—college), it is designed to help them motivate students to learn. These techniques benefit all students, especially those perceived as "low

©1980 Wernher Krutein/PHOTOVAULT

achievers." The program raises the consciousness of educators as to how their behavior and expectations affect the performance of their students and, often, their success or failure. TESA techniques have been successful in dealing with absenteeism, truancy, low morale, lack of motivation, disciplinary concerns, lack of communication, and dropout risks.

- **Special Friends** (Steven R. Carlson, Sanger Unified School District, 1905 7th St., Sanger CA 93657 [209] 875-6521): A primary intervention program of Sanger Unified School District, this program emphasizes early detection of and intervention in school adjustment problems in primary grade students (K—3).

RECOMMENDATION 7

Use the arts to help develop self-esteem and responsibility.

Promote arts programs that stress creative growth as a means of strengthening students' self-esteem and responsibility.

The arts, in their most elemental forms—rhythm, song, dance, drawing, and play acting—are integral to a child's ability to communicate and interact in the world. When the arts become an integrated part of the school curriculum, this familiar language and range of creative activities become powerful resources for learning, communicating, and establishing identity. For students whose academic progress has been slow and who have begun to experience themselves as inadequate, the arts can offer access to the much needed experience of success. Other students find the arts to be an acceptable, nonthreatening way to explore and communicate about their own tumultuous and confusing emotional landscapes.

Another resource developed through artistic skills is an active and disciplined imagination. A healthy self-concept requires strong and focused imaginative powers. The young inexperienced child or adolescent often must *see* or conceptualize his or her strength or ability before being willing to test it.

In his book *Can We Rescue the Arts for America's Children?* Charles Fowler (1989) states: "The arts are basic by any consideration of what addresses our human aesthetic and emotional needs." He feels that a balanced curriculum should be dedicated to achieving "multiple forms of literacy. . . encompassing the symbol system we call the fine arts . . . invented to enable us to react to the world, to analyze it, and to record our impressions so that they can be shared."

The arts also offer young people opportunities to provide a public service by sharing their talents and entertaining and uplifting people's spirits and, thus, be socially responsible.

Some of the exemplary arts programs that were brought to the Task Force's attention were these:

- **Actors Alley** (P. O. Box 8500, Van Nuys, CA 91409 [818] 990-5543): This program sponsors theater troupes going to the schools with an AIDS education program.

- **National Self-Esteem Resource and Development Center—B.E.S.T.** (Believe in Yourself, Empower Yourself, Stand Up for Yourself, Trust Yourself—"The Esteem Team Program"—Judith Feldman, founder, 176 Corte Anita, Greenbrae, CA 94904 [415] 461-3401): This center provides a four-part program consisting of performing, community service, life skills activities, and parent involvement for children (ages six through eleven) in an after school or classroom setting that enhances self-esteem, increases children's sense of independence, and supports the family unit.

- **Social and Public Arts Resource Center** (685 Venice Boulevard, Venice, CA 90291 [213] 822-9560): This program uses visual arts and outdoor murals for the education and affirmation of youth.

RECOMMENDATION 8

Expand counseling and peer counseling services for students.

Enhance growth in self-esteem by developing, supporting, and expanding peer counseling training programs for junior and senior high school students.

Support student self-esteem by encouraging California schools to provide an adequate number of qualified on-site or outreach counselors.

Young people today face a daunting array of problems that threaten their ability to get a good education, retain their physical and psychological health, or reach their full potential as contributing members of society. The obstacles include illiteracy, limited exposure to positive role models, ignorance of alternatives to self-destructive behavior, and a dearth of opportunities to become an active part of something larger than oneself.

School counselors play an essential role in supporting the healthy development of children, yet the statewide ratio of counselors to students is 1 to 409. School districts employ fewer counselors today than they did in 1983.

Traditional resources such as social services agencies, mental health organizations, church and community groups, and counselors are perceived by many youth as unavailable or ineffective, if they are even aware of their existence. As youth move from childhood to adulthood, they increasingly turn to their peers for help in times of crises. Peers represent a vast, often untapped, resource. Through peer counseling programs, youth can be taught to be informed and skillful counselors while at the same time learning how to cope with the difficulties they encounter in their own lives.

In an analysis of 143 adolescent drug prevention programs in 1986, Nancy Tobler found that for the average adolescent, peer programs are dramatically more effective than all the other kinds of counseling programs. Among the problems dealt with are language and cultural barriers, school violence and vandalism, academics, dropout rates, and teenage health issues. In using these skills for oneself or in providing service to others, people also gain a legitimate sense of self-worth and achievement.

Frank Riessman (1987) has stated that peer-mediated processes have many potential benefits: they individualize learning, provide emotional support, reorganize teaching, reorient the teacher-centered classroom, provide more active learning, build self-esteem, and are highly cost effective.

Some of the counseling programs brought to the Task Force's attention are the following:

- **California Peer Counseling Association** (9300 East Imperial Highway OPD, Downey, CA 90242 [818] 308-2331): The mission of this association is to encourage, promote, support, and enhance peer counseling projects in California. The Association's annual conference has grown from 600 in 1985 to 4,000 in 1989. The majority of its members are in the public schools, working with staff and overseeing the work of thousands of youth peer counselors.

- **Peer Helping Association** (Dr. Barbara Varenhorst, 350 Grove Dr., Portola Valley, CA 94028 [415] 851-8001): Dr. Varenhorst is vice-president of the California Peer Counseling Association and the author of several books on the subject. This program is responsible for training trainers by increasing their skills and knowledge. The program has assisted in increasing the number of programs across the state and in strengthening the community network among peer counselors.

- **Peers Helping Peers** (Dr. Milton Wilson, State Department of Education, 721 Capitol Mall, Sacramento, CA 95814 [916] 323-0567): Now in its second year, this program is a unique small project that provides selected school districts with state funds to establish peer counseling or conflict resolution programs in middle or junior high schools. The program is designed to prevent violence and vandalism on campus.

- **Telesis Peer Counseling Program** (Larry Burns, 3180 University Ave., Ste. 640, San Diego, CA 92104 [619] 280-1828): This program provides a comprehensive training process for students in kindergarten through grade twelve, and it promotes the enhancement of sensitive listeners, covering an area from tutoring to crisis intervention.

RECOMMENDATION 9

Provide cooperative learning opportunities.

Encourage the use of cooperative learning in all areas of instruction.

Cooperative learning is a general teaching strategy that can be used with any age group and any subject matter. It is often referred to as *team learning* because students work together in small learning teams. By discussing assignments, conducting experiments, solving problems, writing stories and reports, resolving conflicts, and reaching agreement, students learn important cooperative skills at the same time that they master academic material and learn strategies for thinking, interpreting, and reasoning.

Patterned after positive applications in industry, cooperative learning creatively addresses many of the problems confronting education today: ethnically and academically mixed classrooms, with growing numbers of language minority students; poor motivation and low achievement; negative student attitudes toward school, teachers, and authority in general; and resulting alienation and drop-out. By creating a network of peer support in their cooperative learning groups, students begin taking more responsibility for themselves and each other. Their academic performance improves, and they develop more positive attitudes toward themselves, each other, and school in general.

Cooperative learning strategies are among the best researched innovations within education. Hundreds of studies demonstrate academic, social, and psychological benefits from well-implemented cooperative learning programs, with improved self-esteem and a sense of shared responsibility being important outcomes.

Some examples of cooperative learning programs follow:

• **Child Development Project in San Ramon** (Dr. Marilyn Watson, 111 Deerwood Place, Suite 165, San Ramon, CA 94583 [415] 838-7270): This project is designed to develop social skills in children. It is an elementary school project that has five different components: developing discipline, social understanding through literature, cooperative learning, helping activities, and the development of social values.

• **Cooperative Learning Implementation Project in Redwood City** (Carole Cooper, Professional Development Center, c/o Hoover School, Charter at Stambaugh St., Redwood City, CA 94063 [415] 364-8594): This project has developed models for cooperative learning (high levels of cognitive development balanced with the students' personal needs and social interactions); staff development (two years of in-service training with the teachers to improve their skills); coaching (trainers are involved in the classroom with the teachers); and implementation (work with the entire school over a two-year period to blend cooperative learning into the whole culture of the school).

• **California Association for Cooperation in Education** (Dr. Laurel Robertson, President, Developmental Studies Center, 111 Deerwood Place, Suite 165, San Ramon, CA 94583 [415] 838-7270): This is a statewide association whose members include teachers, administrators, and curriculum developers. The organization publishes a newsletter, conducts workshops, coordinates training, and establishes policy in the development of cooperation in learning.

Reduce class sizes or student: adult ratios.

Every local school board in California should strive to reduce class sizes. Schools in the meantime must use techniques that allow for more individualized attention despite large class sizes.

Having his or her needs addressed, learning thought processes and skills, and having time for personal interaction with teachers are vital to a student's self-esteem and achievement. California has the second largest class sizes in the nation.

Although the Task Force could not find formal research on the correlation between class size and self-esteem, a recent report on class size and academic achievement provides some relevant findings. According to these researchers (McLaughlin, Pfeifer, Swanson-Owens, and Yee, 1986), ". . . research is pretty consistent in showing that smaller classes positively impact teacher classroom attitude and behavior."

A study by Smith and Glass found ". . . even stronger relationships between smaller classes and teacher attitudes, morale, and satisfaction, students' attitudes and interests, and improved classroom practices. In smaller classes, teachers felt better and showed greater use of individualization in instruction, more varied pedagogy, and increased interactions with students."

The passage of Proposition 98 in 1989 provides additional discretionary funding that can be used for classroom aides, staggering starting times, and/or limiting class enrollment. Parents and communities should urge their local school boards to allocate budgets for this important purpose.

Implement programs to counteract bigotry and prejudice.

School districts, with guidance from the State Department of Education, should institute effective programs for staff and students to ensure equality of treatment and opportunity for all.

In spite of gains in the last 20 years, prejudice, bigotry, and discrimination continue to be rampant in our society. The Task Force received considerable testimony regarding the damage these evils inflict on people's self-esteem and lives, and certainly on students' ability to learn.

Acknowledging that there have been significant improvements in the movement toward racial justice, we must also recognize that continuing racial tensions and conflicts constitute a destructive reality in our cities and communities today. There is also evidence that racial discrimination has become more complicated; that is, we now find growing discrimination among a wide assortment of ethnic groups.

The Task Force also heard testimony concerning violent discrimination against lesbian and gay citizens, with the report that such violence has increased since the beginning of the AIDS crisis. In 1988 the National Gay and Lesbian Task Force documented over 7,000 incidents of violence against lesbians and gays, ranging from harassment to homicide.

Discrimination against any person because of perceived differences is totally inconsistent with the fundamental proposition that every human being deserves to be treated with dignity and respect. So long as discrimination against any group continues, no group is safe. The principles of compassion, caring, and understanding must be taught and practiced as part of our efforts to promote personal and social responsibility, as well as responsible character development.

A distinguishing characteristic of the new *History–Social Science Framework*, adopted by the State Board of Education in 1987, is its emphasis on the study of controversy. Teachers are encouraged to use the study of controversial issues, both in history and in current affairs, to teach students that people in a democratic society have the right to disagree, that different perspectives have to be taken into account, and that judgments should be based on reasonable evidence, not on bias and emotion.

The Task Force received information on the following programs designed to counteract bigotry and prejudice:

I get by with a little help from my friends. . . Going to try with a little help from my friends.

—*The Beatles*

- **Desegregation Assistance Center** (Dr. Harriett Doss Willis, SW Regional Laboratory, 4665 Lampson Ave., Los Alamitos, CA 90720 [213] 598-7661): This Federal Title IV funded program delivers services to boards of education in Arizona, California, and Nevada, and it provides information and assistance in dealing with language minority students, race desegregation, and sex equity issues.

- **The Green Circle Program, Inc.** (Dorothy Dorsay, 777 N. First St., Mezzanine, San Jose, CA 95112 [408] 286-9663): This intergroup education program is designed to promote self-esteem and positive intergroup relationships among people of diverse backgrounds. The unique aspect of GCP is a dedication to build a strong network of volunteer facilitators who share a commitment to inter-ethnic respect, understanding, and cooperation and who are able to communicate this message to children as well as to adults.

- **Intergroup Relations/Cultural Inclusion Unit** (Dr. Minta Brown, State Department of Education, 721 Capitol Mall, Sacramento, CA 95814 [916] 323-6353): This group assists school districts in dealing with desegregation, racial conflict, and the social and emotional impacts of California's highly diverse student population.

- **Teacher Education Program** (Dr. Cynthia Lawrence-Wallace, QO70 University of California, San Diego, CA 92093 (619) 534-1680): This program provides interactive workshops in examining personal prejudice and in identifying personal actions to take against racism.

References for Education, Academic Failure, and Self-esteem

Borba, Michele. *Esteem Builders: A K-8 Self-Esteem Curriculum for Improving Student Achievement, Behavior, and School Effectiveness.* Rolling Hills Estates, Calif.: B. L. Winch & Associates, 1989.

Clark, Reginald M. *Family Life and School Achievement: Why Poor Black Children Succeed or Fail.* Evanston: University of Chicago Press, 1983.

Comer, James P. "Parent Participation in the Schools," *Phi Delta Kappan*, (Feb., 1986), 442–446.

Covington, Martin V. "Self-Esteem and Failure in School: Analysis and Policy Implications," in *The Social Importance of Self-Esteem.* Berkeley, Calif.: University of California Press, 1989.

Fowler, Charles. *Can We Rescue the Arts for America's Children?* New York: American Council for the Arts, 1989.

Here They Come: Ready or Not. Sacramento, Calif.: California State Department of Education, 1988.

Jones, J. G., and L. Grieneeks. "Measures of Self-Perception as Predictors of Scholastic Achievement," *Journal of Educational Research*, Vol. 63, No. 5 (1970), 201–203.

McLaughlin, Milbrey W., R. Scott Pfeifer, Deborah Swanson-Owens, and Sylvia Yee. "Why Teachers Won't Teach," *Phi Delta Kappan*, Vol. 56 (1986), 420–426.

Moore, R. S., and D. Moore. "When Education Becomes Abuse: A Different Look at the Mental Health of Children," *Journal of School Health*, Vol. 2 (1986), 56, 73–74.

Riessman, Frank. "The New Peer Wave: Why Now?" *Peer Facilitators' Quarterly*, Vol. 5, No. 4 (Sept., 1987), 6.

Tobler, Nancy. "Meta-Analysis of 143 Drug Prevention Programs," *Journal of Drug Issues*, Vol. 16, No. 4 (1986).

Walberg, H. J., "Families as Partners in Educational Productivity," *Phi Delta Kappan*, Vol. 65, No. 6. (Feb., 1984), 397–400.

Drug and Alcohol Abuse and Self-esteem

Alcohol and drug abuse, long a problem in Western societies, has become a paramount concern in our times. Some facts highlight the urgent need to move effectively to solve the problem (statistics taken from: Kitano, et al., 1989, and "Indicators of Alcohol and Drug Abuse Trends," published by the Department of Alcohol and Drug Abuse Programs):

Alcohol

- A 1983 study estimated 18 million adults nationally experienced problems from alcohol use—and 10.6 million were alcoholics.
- Two-thirds of the adult population drink; but of that group, the 10 percent who drink most heavily drink half of the total alcohol consumed nationally.
- In California, 2.2 million people (almost 8 percent of the population) experience problems with alcohol.
- Alcohol is a factor in nearly half of all accidental deaths, suicides, and homicides, and in 42 percent of all deaths from motor vehicle accidents.
- During 1987, a total of 4,443 emergency room episodes involving alcohol in combination with some other drug were reported by a sample of hospitals in the Los Angeles, San Francisco, and San Diego areas alone.

Drugs

- Approximately 2.1 million persons in California use illicit drugs or misuse legal drugs.
- In California, 222,000 people use drugs intravenously, increasing the risk of spreading AIDS.
- An estimated 3 million Americans are addicted to cocaine.
- An estimated 10 percent of those who have ever used cocaine become addicts, and they consume 75 percent of the cocaine used in the United States.
- Perhaps 450,000 Californians are addicted to cocaine, many to the highly addictive smokable form called crack.

Crime

- Almost two out of three persons arrested for any felony in Los Angeles tested positive for cocaine. Arrestees often test positive for multiple (poly) drug use, including combinations with alcohol.

- In 1985, a study concluded that almost half of the persons in prison had been under the influence of alcohol at the time the criminal offense was committed.
- Heroin addicts are estimated to engage in criminal activities for about half the days in a year.
- Over three out of every four persons arrested for a felony in San Diego and Los Angeles recently tested positive for an illegal drug other than marijuana.
- In 1989 for the first time in California's history, felony drug arrests became the single largest crime category, surpassing property arrests.

Cost

- Far more than dollar costs are involved, but these alone are staggering. Annual costs for Californians are estimated to be:

  $ 11.7 billion for alcohol abuse

  <u>6.0</u> billion for drug abuse

  $ 17.7 billion total

- For purposes of comparison, the total budget for state government in California is approximately $50 billion.
- These total costs each year equal $631 for every man, woman, and child living in California.
- Based on a 1985 study, each dollar lost on alcohol and drugs was due to:

	Alcohol	*Drugs*
Lost productivity	$ .57	$ .60
Crime, welfare, social welfare	.12	.32
Treatment and support	.12	.03
Deaths	.15	.04
Lost jobs	.04	.01

- Health care costs nationally for accidents and illnesses related to alcohol abuse were estimated at $15 billion in 1983.
- These dollar costs do not take into account the enormous social costs of marital problems, violence against children and spouses, or the emotional trauma of living with drug or alcohol addicts.

Effect of Alcohol and Drug Abuse on Children

Of additional and considerable concern is the widespread appearance of drug-addicted babies. State statistics indicate that 5 to 8 percent of women of childbearing age are drug and alcohol dependent; 2 to 3 percent are cocaine dependent; and 0.5 percent are heroin or methadone dependent (Kirst, et al., 1989). Among those arrested for felonies, women in some cities test positive for cocaine at higher rates than men.

Not surprisingly, drug addicted babies are being born at unprecedented rates. Press reports indicate that up to 25 percent of the babies born at some Los Angeles and Bay Area hospitals are addicted to crack; in Sacramento, 25 percent of the infant intensive care admissions involve drug addiction ("Children's Agenda 1989-90," Child Abuse Council of Sacramento, 1989).

Cocaine abuse by pregnant women is associated with low birth weight, premature birth or abortion, and retardation of growth before birth. Infants often display tremors, muscular rigidity, rapid breathing, irritability, jitteriness, and poor control. There are no studies on the long-term effects of cocaine or crack on children, but most professionals anticipate that such effects as mental retardation, social difficulties, hyperactivity, and poor learning capacities are probable (Child Abuse Council of Sacramento, 1989).

Infants who are exposed to alcohol and other drugs may suffer permanent neurological damage, exhibiting delays in development and speech, impaired motor development, inability to enjoy ordinary childhood activities, and difficulty in interpersonal relationships. Inner-city day-care workers report growing populations of children with garbled speech who cannot sit still or play with other children (Kirst, et al., 1989).

The remainder of this century and the early quarter of the next will see major challenges to the education, health, welfare, judicial, and hospital systems as drug-addicted babies grow up.

Children suffer lifelong consequences when raised in homes with adults addicted to alcohol or other drugs. A major outgrowth of the Alcoholics Anonymous programs has been the Adult Children of Alcoholics, an extension of Twelve-Step assistance to those raised in addicted homes. Studies during the mid 1970s demonstrated that children raised in alcoholic homes scored significantly lower on measures of self-concept than adolescents from nonalcoholic homes did. Children from alcoholic homes often exhibit excessive dependency, emotional insecurity, feelings of isolation and guilt, and an inability to express emotions (Black, 1979).

Recent research suggests that some (perhaps many) people are biologically susceptible to depression, including overpowering feelings of self-worthlessness which sometimes lead to suicide. Other inquiries are beginning to document the biological and genetic susceptibilities to alcohol and drug abuse among some individuals. Though this work is too new to permit firm conclusions, the two lines of research may be related as they affect the same areas of the brain. Moreover, some of the new antidepressants have been helpful in treating addiction (Restak, 1988).

We have only to look at our media images to find that our culture has promoted drug and alcohol use. During recent decades, movies have depicted drug use as fashionable fun, though this has changed dramatically as the consequences of addiction have become well

... our own willful impulses can become a rich source of renewal of imaginative powers.

—*Sheldon Kopp*

known. For most of American history, advertising has effectively sold patented medications as panaceas for an astonishing range of human ills; the first cycles of cocaine and opiate addiction in the United States resulted from widespread promotion of those drugs. Today, alcohol remains a major topic of advertising, especially to the young.

Self-esteem and Substance Abuse

... the [child's] sense of autonomy is a reflection of the parents' dignity as autonomous beings.

—Erik Erikson

Even more than research into the links between other social problems and self-esteem, substance abuse research is greatly flawed by inconsistent and incorrect definitions of self-esteem. Compounding this problem is the fact that by its very nature, drug abuse is secret and difficult to measure. Alcoholics also take elaborate measures to hide their abuse, making research difficult.

Many studies show clear, though sometimes indirect, links between self-esteem and substance abuse. Others are unable to document a connection, and some even assert increases in self-esteem resulting from substance abuse. These latter studies illustrate well the drawbacks of simplistic measures of self-esteem: those who drink to excess or abuse drugs to "feel good" may temporarily and superficially inflate their perceptions of self, while adding to a deeper problem. As researchers Skager and Kerst (1989) found:

> Pumping up a flat tire is an inappropriate analogy for recovery from an addiction. Rather, an internalized capability to generate self-esteem has to be developed. Recovery is no magic trick. It requires hard work in the service of significant personal development.

But research does solidly document a connection between substance abuse and self-*concept*, a broader notion which includes self-esteem (the experience of one's personal worth) (Skager et al., 1989). Psychological theory suggests that a failure to develop a healthy concept of one's self, either very early in childhood or in later relationships with parents, can create a condition ripe for drug and alcohol abuse:

> The addictive use of alcohol or drugs may be viewed as an abortive attempt to recreate a primitive mental state, from which interrupted growth can begin again anew. Addiction, of course, is a flawed solution. (Skager, et al., 1989)

These same authors conclude that "There is no doubt that self-esteem is central in the consciousness of troubled human beings . . . this applies equally well to the alcoholic." (Skager, et al., 1989) Alcoholics Anonymous describe the mental state of the alcoholic as "pitiful and incomprehensible demoralization." Hitting bottom for the alcoholic is a state of negative self-worth, a vacuum in which self-denegration replaces self-esteem.

Some research confirms the connection between self-esteem and substance abuse but is unable to distinguish cause and effect. Does the addiction cause the low self-esteem, or vice versa? At least one major study (Steffenhagen and Burns, 1987) concluded that low levels of self-esteem are the cause, not the result, of deviant behavior: "In other words, alcoholics or drug addicts behave as they do because of low self-esteem, rather than developing low self-esteem as the result of deviant behavior." (Kitano, 1989)

Recovery from Substance Abuse: Rebuilding Self-esteem

For two decades, low self-esteem has been the most popular psychological explanation for substance abuse and addiction; and rebuilding it, the almost universal requirement for recovery.

Recovery, denial, relapse are beyond the scope of this discussion, but several aspects deserve elaboration here.

It is clear that true recovery requires a complex reconstruction of personality structures:

> *Low self-esteem is not susceptible to a quick fix, as is often assumed in prevention programs for young people. Rather, lasting enhancement of self-esteem requires the development of a positive and rigorous self-concept or identity. In the case of alcoholics and other addicts, this process requires significant changes in personality organization and associated systems of values. (Skager, et al., 1989)*

One study looked closely at a group of addicts who "cured" themselves without formal treatment. The single conclusion stemming from the analysis is that "to change their lives . . . addicts must fashion new identities, perspectives, and social world involvement wherein the addict identity is excluded or dramatically depreciated." (Biernacki, 1986)

The interconnections between substance abuse and responsibility are many and complex. Psychological theory holds that those suffering low self-esteem also experience a wide gap between their *ideal self* (what they think they should be) and their *perceived self* (what they think they are). When this gap is too wide, they suffer grave doubts and self-hatred. One study (MacAndrew, 1979) concluded that drunkenness allowed alcoholics to dispense with any concern about accountability that might be associated with their sober selves and to express resentment without feeling anxious.

The social aspects of self-esteem are an important part of understanding the connection with substance abuse and any recovery:

> *If children are accepted, approved, and respected for what they are, they will most likely acquire attitudes of self-esteem and self-acceptance. But if the significant people in their lives belittle, blame, and reject them, they are likely to evolve unfavorable self-attitudes. On the whole, social psychological research has supported the overall postulate that we hold the keys to one another's self-conceptions and identities. (Kitano, 1989)*

In short, we are individually and collectively responsible for our dealings with others, particularly children, and the consequences of those dealings to self-esteem.

The norms of a group strongly affect both the extent of drug and alcohol abuse and the "general self-esteem" of its members. Rates of drug and alcohol abuse vary tremendously among various ethnic and cultural groups, and one of the factors thought to influence this variation is the attitude of the group toward drugs and alcohol. A 1980 study by Perez among Mexican-American youth in East Los Angeles concluded that use was "clearly shown to be affected not only by sociodemographic and cultural variables but also by self-concept factors."

The relationship among cultural attitudes, substance abuse, and self-esteem are quite complicated and not well understood. It seems likely that more is involved than cultural values which reflect directly on drunkenness. For example, parenting practices within a culture may foster healthy self-concepts, leading to lower rates of substance abuse.

Finally, some researchers theorize that racism and animosity among large cultural subgroups can affect the self-esteem of individuals in the group and perhaps contribute to substance abuse problems. Low self-esteem may be experienced by a member of an ethnic or cultural minority that is stereotyped in a negative way and who further suffers inequality in economic, political, and social ways.

Summary to Drug and Alcohol Abuse and Self-esteem

Once the self-concept changes, behavior changes to match the freshly perceived self.

—*Carl Rogers*

Alcohol and drug abuse stem from multiple sources; there is no single cause of substance abuse. Self-esteem is an important part of self-concept. A poor self-concept often contributes to addiction. Conversely, recovering from addiction by rebuilding one's identity requires a growth in genuine self-esteem.

These observations suggest that superficial attempts to enhance self-esteem, including such tactics as enhancing highly specific performance capabilities or giving empty praise for minor accomplishments, are not enough to treat or prevent the abuse of alcohol or other drugs. In a letter to the Task Force, Professor Skager summed it up this way:

> *The prevention and treatment of alcohol and drug abuse should focus on the development of a healthy sense of self . . . that is capable of sustaining self-esteem through the normal problems of living, accompanied by a parallel development in related personal values and choices of drug-free social involvements.*

Individuals make choices that affect their own well-being and that of the community. Despite the causes or forces that contribute to substance abuse, the decision to drink or *do* drugs is as individual as the decision to seek treatment or to discourage substance abuse. Personal and social responsibility are required to build self-esteem. Further, our cultural values affect healthy self-esteem, including good parental practices, and are as important as healthy attitudes toward abuse of drugs and alcohol.

©1983 Wernher Krutein/PHOTOVAULT

Key Recommmendations on Drug and Alcohol Abuse and Self-esteem

1. Local officials should develop community-based substance abuse prevention councils that, in addition to overseeing local prevention efforts, simultaneously promote self-esteem and personal and social responsibility.
2. Expand and support treatment programs for substance abusers by replicating successful programs.

Recommendations on Drug and Alcohol Abuse and Self-esteem in Brief Form

1. Create prevention councils in every community.
2. Expand treatment programs.
3. Create culturally sensitive prevention strategies.
4. Educate parents.
5. Expand school prevention programs.
6. Encourage responsible media.

Recommendations, Discussion, and Program Examples on Drug and Alcohol Abuse and Self-esteem

Create prevention councils in every community.

Local officials should develop community-based substance abuse prevention councils that, in addition to overseeing local prevention efforts, simultaneously promote self-esteem and personal and social responsibility.

Prevention councils work with government agencies, schools, businesses, and community members to affect public policy regarding alternatives to drug and alcohol abuse. These councils promote self-esteem within the community by empowering people to make important changes in their lives and in their communities. Activities include mobilizing existing and potential resources, creating information centers, and focusing attention on the needs of minorities and other underserved groups. Other suggested functions for these councils include planning and coordinating prevention activities, promoting innovative programs, developing stable funding sources, and disseminating current information. Institutions within the private sector, including alcohol-related industries, are strongly urged to assist in the funding of these programs.

- **Friday Night Live** (111 Capitol Mall, Room 223, Sacramento, CA 95814, [916] 445-7456): This is a student-centered program that works with teenagers to reverse the pressure to use alcohol and other drugs. FNL works within the whole community. It does not lecture. It helps students to share with, and influence, other students. With the ongoing support and guidance of FNL, thousands of teenagers from different social and ethnic backgrounds are finding that they can join together to influence their peers, communities, and society through fun, action-oriented chapters and events.

- **Campaign for a Healthier Community for Children** (1000 Sir Francis Drake Blvd., Room 10, San Anselmo, CA 94960, [415] 456-7693): This program's aim is to assist people in transforming their world. More caring relationships between people, and between people and the world they live in, are the guiding principles. The Campaign's goals are:

1. To assist people in creating their *families* of friends and neighbors in an intergenerational pattern
2. To encourage adults to take responsibility for the community's children

3. To give support to parents
4. To return older people to their significant place in the community
5. To reestablish significant roles for children and youth in the community's daily life

The Campaign establishes councils in which volunteers of all ages carry out a variety of projects and activities to achieve these goals in each community.

- **Twelve Step programs**: Twelve-Step programs (based on the Alcoholics Anonymous model) represent the backbone of effective treatment and the self-help movement. They exemplify the four criteria of an affirming environment: a sense of belonging, of significance, of liking themselves and being liked, and an appreciation of hard work. These programs are built around self-acceptance, spiritual awareness, personal responsibility, and nonjudgmental group support.

RECOMMENDATION 2

Expand treatment programs.

Expand and support treatment programs for substance abusers by replicating successful programs.

Local program developers and providers have the advantage of understanding their community's special problems, needs, customs, and norms. They thus may be able to contact otherwise hard-to-reach populations suffering from alcohol and drug abuse. In addition to community-based centers, however, numerous private and private nonprofit organizations, hospitals, and clinics incorporate self-esteem enhancement in their treatment programs. There is a sad lack of programs for many groups, including adolescents, some minorities, and some women.

- **Delancey Street Foundation** (2563 Divisadero St., San Francisco, CA 94115 [415] 563-5326): A self-help residential treatment center for recovering addicts, alcoholics, ex-convicts, and ex-prostitutes, this foundation helps people find their strengths, improve their weaknesses, and generally enhance their self-esteem. The program is designed to stop crime and the abuse of drugs and alcohol. It also teaches people the skills and values they need to live legitimately and successfully in society.

Residents are tutored to receive a high school equivalency certificate. Advanced schooling (e.g., arts, real estate, medical and technical sciences) is also available. Residents must receive vocational training in at least three marketable skills in the foundation's ten training schools. They also must attend daily seminars and group therapy. They are involved in a variety of community service projects, including aid to seniors and the handicapped, crime prevention programs with the police and area businesses, and youth drug abuse prevention. The program stresses discipline, decency and dignity, self-respect through working hard, and reaching out to serve others as a way to feel good about oneself.

- **3HO SuperHealth** (2545 N. Woodland Rd., Tucson, AZ 85749 [602] 749-0404): A private organization accredited by the American Medical Association's Joint Commission on Accreditation of Hospitals, this group is a prevention and rehabilitation program designed to teach people a holistic approach to health-related behavior. 3HO offers a comprehensive approach to treatment (alcohol and chemical dependency, co-dependency, stress management, smoking cessation, weight loss, fitness) through physical vitality, mental stability, and spiritual health based in part on the teachings of Kundalini Yoga and meditation. Clients learn healthy life-style skills that promote wellness and stability. Staff members help formulate after-care programs to sustain continued progress.

RECOMMENDATION 3

Create culturally sensitive prevention strategies.

Design, support, and expand culturally sensitive drug and alcohol prevention strategies that serve the unique needs of California's ethnic and other cultural populations.

To be effective, prevention programs must be sensitive to the target population's family structure and value system and to the community's development and history. It is especially important for these programs to relate to the underlying problems of poverty, societal deprivation, and the environmental conditions. Program planning must involve members of the targeted community. Materials should be consistent with the language, style, and customs of the community. The history of the community—migration, immigration, urban renewal, industrial housing—will influence the degree of receptiveness the local population demonstrates for prevention efforts. Each community, however, must finally take responsibility for itself.

- **Didi Hirsch Community Mental Health Center** (Dr. Ann Lodwig Brand, 4760 S. Sepulveda Blvd., Culver City, CA 90230, (213) 390-6612): This Los Angeles County project focuses on reducing the availability of alcohol to black and Hispanic youth in the Venice/Oakwood area. The project brings together youth, adults, school personnel, business, and other community leaders to establish an Alcohol Prevention Action Coalition and to develop a community action plan.

- **International Child Resource Institute** (Kenneth Jaffe, 1810 Hopkins St., Berkeley, CA 94707, (415) 644-1000): This Alameda County project will develop, field test, and distribute a primary prevention program designed to prevent alcohol-related problems among California's Hispanic youth. The program will promote self-esteem and personal development of preschool and early-school-age children who are being cared for by day-care providers.

- **Tule River Indian Health Program** (Nancy McDarmet, P.O. Box 589, Porterville, CA 93258, (209) 781-4271): This Tulare County project targets Native American women and adolescents to provide peer support and alcohol education and training. Program participants become permanent, knowledgeable voluntary support members within families and among peers throughout the Indian community.

- **North of Market Senior Women's Alcohol Program** (Vera Haile, 333 Turk St., San Francisco, CA 94102, (415) 885-2274): The goal of this San Francisco County project is to reach out to isolated older women alcoholics of the North-of-Market area, to provide recreational activities and an ongoing support group, and to generate more women's participation in treatment for low-income women who live alone without family support.

- **Project Opportunity, Mother Lode Women's Center** (P.O. Box 633, Sonora, CA 95370, (209) 532-4746): In response to the growing problems of female drug dependency, and in the belief that women develop chemical dependency problems in response to stressful life events more frequently than men do, this prevention program works to build self-esteem during these critical times.

RECOMMENDATION 4

Educate parents.

Educate parents about the dangers of drugs and encourage them to assume personal responsibility for substance abuse prevention within their family.

The family is the most important unit for transmitting values, mores, and attitudes. To prevent their children from becoming involved with drugs, parents must have a way to obtain the necessary skills and knowledge. They also need the opportunity to gain help for their own substance abuse problems. Parents must have access to information and training regarding the effects of drugs, signs of drug use, parental responsibility, communication techniques, empowerment strategies, and parental skills. Parental support systems and drug-free activity centers should be made available, and special efforts must be made to reach high-risk populations.

- **Parenting Strategies for Drug Abuse Prevention** (Kerby Alvey, Ph.D., Center for the Improvement of Child Caring, 11331 Ventura Blvd., Suite 103, Studio City, CA 91406, [818] 980-0903): This program provides Training for Trainers (TOT) sessions on two culturally adapted versions of effectiveness training for parents that focus on black and Hispanic families. The TOT sessions will be conducted for drug prevention practitioners.

- **The Confident Parenting Program** (Michelle Mickiewicz, 300 N. San Antonio Rd., Santa Barbara, CA 93110, [805] 681-5440): The Santa Barbara County Office of Substance Abuse sponsors this program, designed to provide parents with the support and skills that enable them to develop strong, supportive relationships with their children. Research has shown that members of families that have close supportive relationships are less likely to experience serious or lasting problems with drugs.

RECOMMENDATION 5

Expand school prevention programs.

Support and enhance prevention programs in the schools with the goals of reducing substance abuse, building self-esteem, and enhancing healthy character development.

Although substance abuse is certainly affected by the availability of substances, only the fading of demand will protect us from the consequences of abuse. If individuals with high self-esteem choose other, more successful and long-lasting ways to deal with life's difficulties, there would be less need for enforcement interventions. Building self-esteem, character, and competence in our youngsters can play a critical role in reducing demand.

While the family is the primary sphere of influence, schools are also powerful socializing agents. Their access to children in kindergarten through grade twelve provides a unique opportunity to teach and model the prevention of substance abuse and abstinence from drug use.

The programs taught in our schools must follow a sequence that parallels the age and experience of the students. The messages of developing character and responsibility, making healthy life-style and behavioral choices, and learning to take control over one's health and actions should all be part of a comprehensive substance abuse program.

The curriculum and materials are important, but the role of the teacher and school staff is vital. Initial training should be provided for the entire school staff. More specialized training for classroom staff should be provided on an ongoing basis so that teachers are up-to-date and refreshed.

Part of the choice of the curricula should be an examination of "risk factors." Certain of our children enter school already at risk of social and academic failure. Often they are the children of alcoholics and drug users, the children from disorderly or impoverished homes; and they need attention immediately. Too often the warning signs are ignored, and eventually the judicial system is the first to focus on these children when it is too late.

Programs and curriculum for these youth need to include parents and families. This is difficult, but communities can do it. Indeed, some are doing it.

• **Character and Personal Responsibility Education** (Thomas Jefferson Center, 202 S. Lake Ave., Suite 240, Pasadena, CA 91101 [818] 792- 8130): This program provides classroom posters and curriculum that are designed to teach specific skills for decision making, goal setting, and accepting responsibility for one's behavior. The underlying principle is that the primary prevention of drug and alcohol abuse is based on acquiring personal and social responsibility skills as the foundation for high self-esteem.

- **DARE** (Drug Abuse Resistance Education) (3353 San Fernando Rd., Los Angeles, CA 90028, [213] 485-4856): Created by the Los Angeles Police Department in cooperation with the Los Angeles Unified School District, this very successful program equips fifth- and sixth-grade students with life skills for resisting peer pressure to experiment with drugs and alcohol. The curriculum focuses on techniques of peer pressure resistance, self-management skills, self-concept improvement, and value decisions concerning respect for the law and personal safety. In addition to significant gains in tested abilities to deal with drug-oriented situations, 50 percent of the DARE students increased their grade point averages, approximately one-third by more than half a grade point and 12 percent by a full grade point or more.

- **Here's Looking at You 2000** (Comprehensive Health Education Foundation, 22323 Pacific Highway South, Seattle, WA 98198, [206] 824-2907): Designed to prevent alcohol and drug abuse through education and enhanced self-esteem, this comprehensive drug curriculum includes extensive information about the negative effects of drugs as well as numerous lessons on building self-esteem.

- **SANE** (Substance Abuse Narcotics Education) (11515 S. Colima Rd., Bldg. D-111, Whittier, CA 90604 [213] 946-SANE): This successful law enforcement sponsored program, developed by the Los Angeles Sheriff's Department in partnership with 50 school districts, addresses the demand for drugs while teaching students self-esteem and decision-making skills (including personal responsibility for decisions), how to deal with peer pressure, and general information about the effect of drugs on the body and mind. Law enforcement officers and teachers work together to develop and deliver a curriculum. The police also work with parents and churches, community groups, and service organizations. The program targets fourth-, fifth-, and sixth-grade students and is expanding to include younger and older groups. SANE recently initiated a new high school program entitled "Drugs, Pregnancy, and You," designed to teach students about the damage that occurs to the fetus when drugs and alcohol are used during pregnancy.

RECOMMENDATION 6

Encourage responsible media.

Encourage the various commercial media to recognize and develop social responsibility in presenting information to Americans and influencing public values, particularly those affecting drugs and alcohol use.

Media greatly affect our personal lives and self-esteem. They choose the facts and images that shape our understanding of the world, its groups, life styles, and occupations. These choices can be informative, but the need to simplify information can also, implicitly or explicitly, perpetuate racial, ethnic, and sexual stereotypes. Dick Cable, TV news anchorman for KXTV, Sacramento, said:

> ... because so much of the way we define ourselves as a people is from the images returning from the television screen ... I think we may rightfully assume, and perhaps even demand, that imperfect mirror that we watch ourselves in has the primary responsibility in the end for creating a healthy climate of self-esteem.

Television, radio, movies, newspapers, and magazines are highly influential in setting the agenda and tone for public and private discussions. Through the news, entertainment, and advertising they select, our media influence our self-esteem, opinions, and overall outlooks. This is especially true of the young, who seek role models and information about how the world operates.

Entertainment programs and advertising often carry hidden, even unintended, messages. While parents and schools teach reason and discussion, media often portray and glorify *real men* who speak with fists, brawn, and guns—and women who are valued for their looks and superficial sophistication.

The media have assumed some functions once reserved for schools, churches, and parents. They teach in a very real sense, providing values for good or ill, as well as information.

For most Californians, the media are major trendsetters and definers of reality. What is not covered is as important as what is. Many newspapers in our huge impersonal urban areas have stopped the tradition of reporting the names of young people who achieve in school or are otherwise recognized by their communities, depriving them of the self-esteem experience of seeing their positive achievements recognized in print. Young gang members, criminals, and athletes are covered at a length disproportionate to their activities.

Not long ago, drug use was often portrayed in movies and other media as fun, creative, and interesting. Those images are now quickly changing as movies portray drug abuse (and cigarette smoking) in a darker light. Similar attention should be paid to:

- The advertising of legal drugs, especially alcohol
- The peer pressure that spreads illegal drug use, the social conditions that spawn it, and the ways it can be treated
- The ethnic, cultural, and sexual stereotypes that harm self-esteem and our esteem of other people

References for Drug and Alcohol Abuse and Self-esteem

Biernacki, P. *Pathways from Heroin Addiction: Recovery Without Treatment.* Philadelphia: Temple University Press, 1986.

Black, Claudia. "Children of Alcoholics," *Alcohol Health and Research World,* Fall, 1979.

"Children's Agenda 1989-90." Sacramento, Calif.: Child Abuse Council of Sacramento, 1989.

Garbarino, J., and M. C. Plantz. "Child Abuse and Juvenile Delinquency: What Are the Links?" in *Troubled Youth, Troubled Families.* New York: Aldine De Gruyter, 1986.

"Indicators of Alcohol and Drug Abuse Trends," in *Five Year Master Plan to Reduce Drug and Alcohol Abuse: Year One.* Sacramento, Calif.: Department of Alcohol and Drug Abuse Programs, 1989.

Kirst, Michael, et al. *Conditions of Children in California.* Berkeley, Calif.: Policy Analysis for California Education, University of California, Berkeley, 1989.

Kitano, Harry H. L. "Alcohol and Drug Use and Self-Esteem: A Sociocultural Perspective," in *The Social Importance of Self-Esteem.* Berkeley, Calif.: University of California Press, 1989.

MacAndrew, C. "A Retrospective Study of Drunkenness: Associated Change in the Self-Depictions of a Large Sample of Male Outpatient Alcoholics," *Addictive Behaviors,* Vol. 4 (1979), 373–381.

Miller, D. *Children of Alcoholics: A Twenty-Year Longitudinal Study.* San Francisco: Institute of Scientific Analysis, 1977.

Perez, R., A. Ramirez, and M. Rodrequez. "Correlates and Changes over Time in Drug and Alcohol Use Within a Barrio Population," *American Journal of Community Psychology,* Vol. 8 (1980), 621–636.

Restak, Richard M. *The Mind.* New York: Bantam Books, 1988.

Schlossman, P. *Cocaine and Heroin in California: The Changing Equation.* Prepared for the Office of the Attorney General, Department of Justice, State of California (in progress, 1989).

Skager, Rodney, and Elizabeth Kerst. "Alcohol and Drug Use: A Psychological Perspective," in *The Social Importance of Self-Esteem.* Berkeley, Calif.: University of California Press, 1989.

Steffenhagen, R.A., and Jeff D. Burns. *The Social Dynamics of Self-Esteem: Theory to Therapy.* New York: Praeger, 1987.

Crime and Violence and Self-esteem

Crime, or the fear of crime, is one of the most pervasive problems facing the citizens of California today. In 1988 more than a quarter of a million homes were burglarized. California suffered almost 3,000 homicides in 1988 and nearly 12,000 reported rapes ("Crime and Deliquency in California," 1988). According to the Los Angeles County Sheriff's Department, 452 persons died because of gang violence in 1988 in that county alone. Crime, and especially violent crime, has become so commonplace and so frequently reported by the media that many citizens have adjusted their daily lives to accommodate the problem.

The roots of crime and violence are many and interrelated. Various theories point to economic, political, cultural, psychological, and moral causes. Many theorists also include the factor of self-concept in their explanations, assuming that people's behavior is influenced by the way they see and feel about themselves. Most social scientists hold a person's self-concept to be the result of his or her socialization or social interaction, especially with important others.

Self-esteem may be a critical issue in violent crimes, particularly violence toward intimates. These crimes are typically generated by intense emotions. The specific notion of self-esteem as a determinant of criminal or violent behavior has resulted in studies seeking to link antecedent levels of self-esteem with subsequent aggression, as well as with other forms of deviant or antisocial behavior.

Relation of Self-esteem to Aggression and Criminal Behavior

Patrick Purdy grew up in a disturbed family setting, badly damaged by the lack of supporting parents. He became a young man with virtually no self-esteem and a high level of anger at the world around him.

—*Report to Attorney General John K. Van de Kamp on Patrick Purdy and the Cleveland School Killings–October 1989*

Research demonstrates the influence of environmental conditioning on self-esteem and thus on aggressive behavior. More specifically, research over the past 20 years into the effects of child abuse indicates a causal relationship between abuse, neglect, and emotional deprivation and juvenile delinquency. In such people, crime and violence may become ways to compensate for feeling shameful, powerless and worthless; these may be desperate attempts to gain power and esteem. In addition, children treated violently by their caregivers learn that violence is an acceptable reaction to conflict and frustration, and they adopt this behavior as adults.

In one study, researchers observed the home lives of three groups of young men, beginning when they were nineteen and continuing for five years. The three classifications were: aggressive, assertive, and nonaggressive (McCord, et al., 1961). They found that the young men who had experienced significantly higher levels of direct parental attacks (physical abuse, verbal threats of punishment or abandonment, derogation, and rejection) as more aggressive than the young men in either of the other groups. The emotional family climate of the aggressive young men tended to undermine their concepts of themselves as people of worth, directly attacked their sense of security, and carried the implications that the world is a dangerous and hostile place.

Many studies of aggression conducted in the late 1930s (Dollard, et al., 1939) centered around a "frustration-aggression" hypothesis. This viewed aggression as a behavioral response to any stimulus that blocked "goal-directed" activity (i.e., the attempt to gain a valued reward such as money, food, or social approval). This research suggests that individuals differ in their predispositions to anger and aggression and, therefore, presumably, in their susceptibility to frustration. Such differences, according to this school of thought, are the product of the individual's self-concept, which includes self-esteem.

Other studies indicate that personal insult (Green, 1968) or an individual's perception of an opponent's aggressive intent (Epstein and Taylor, 1967) are more potent instigators of aggression than frustration per se. Seymour Feshbach (1971) claims that, based on all the experimental and clinical evidence, "violations to self-esteem through insult, humiliation, or coercion are . . . probably the most important source of anger and aggressive drive in humans."

Self-esteem, Pride, and Shame

After reviewing the crime and violence literature for the Task Force, T. J. Scheff and others (1989) suggest that perhaps what is needed is a new direction in research and public policy. This new approach explores the importance of self-esteem in the causation of violent crimes, and it would conceptualize self-esteem in terms of the basic emotions of pride and shame. It could also highlight the environmental components that promote self-esteem and encourage taking personal responsibility for one's own actions.

Early Nurturing. A longitudinal experiment conducted by the Syracuse University Family Development Research Program (Lally, et al., 1987) helps demonstrate the causal role self-esteem may play in violent or criminal behavior. The program attempted to improve the "well-being" of children born into families unable to provide the benefits associated with money, education, and job status. It hoped to bolster family and child functioning. Researchers recruited 108 low-income families to receive a full complement of educational, nutritional, health, safety, and human service resources, beginning prenatally and continuing until the children were of elementary-school age. Self-esteem was also promoted:

> . . . the children involved with this program were treated as special creations, each with particular skills and specialties that would be

appreciated by and useful to the larger society; these special powers were protected and allowed to rise to the ascendence by the adults who spent the daytime hours with them. . . . the context that was fostered set a daily tone of freedom of choice and awareness of responsibility; an expectation of success in each child; confidence in the fairness and consistency of the environment; an emphasis on creativity, excitement, and exploration in learning; expectation of internal rather than external motivation; and a safe, cheerful place to spend each day.

A follow-up study found that the program had positively and significantly affected the participants. One of the strongest indicators was the area of social deviance and ability to function in the community. The findings demonstrated that high-quality early childhood programs prevent the incidence and severity of juvenile delinquency in children from low-income communities.

Ten years after the program ended, only 6 percent of its participants had been processed by the County Probation Office, as compared to 22 percent in a control group. The severity of the offenses, the degree of recidivism, and the cost of the cases (court processing, probation supervision, placement in foster care, etc.) were ten times higher in the control group.

Moreover, program participants tended to express positive feelings about themselves, take an active approach to personal problems, and see schooling as an important part of their lives. The program appeared to prevent severely deviant behavior and also to foster more positive attitudes and values.

A recent report to the Attorney General of California on the tragic killing in a schoolyard in Stockton, in which six children were murdered with semiautomatic weapons, documented the connection between the killer's upbringing, his well diagnosed lack of self-esteem, and his final acts of violence ("Report to Attorney General," 1989).

Deviancy Based Self-confidence. Howard B. Kaplan's "esteem-enhancement" model of deviance (1975, 1980) is one of the most thorough theoretical discussions of the relationship between self-esteem and criminal behavior. In a comprehensive longitudinal study, Mr. Kaplan proposed that delinquent behavior enhances self-confidence for individuals who have experienced failure and a lowered sense of self-worth. This theory assumes a form of self-esteem very different from that promoted by the Task Force. For the purpose of his study, Kaplan defined self-esteem as "the personal need to maximize the experience of positive self-attitudes and to minimize the experience of negative self-attitudes."

Accordingly, when an individual's past experiences in a particular group (family or school, for example) lead to negative self-attitudes, then the individual associates that group with self-derogating experiences and loses the motivation to conform to normative expectations. Deviance then becomes attractive to the extent that it represents opportunities for self-enhancing experiences. Whether deviant

Logic alone should have convinced us that we must devote our attention to the youth at the front end—to delinquency prevention, truancy, drug and alcohol abuse, and gang prevention.

—California Juvenile Justice, Analysis and Legislative Action–January, 1989–Criminal Justice Legal Foundation, Sacramento

behavior is adopted and, if so, which type, depends on what deviant activities are visible, available, and attractive to the particular individual. Whether the deviant activity is continued depends in turn on the extent to which the person feels it is self-enhancing or self-derogating.

An important example of the esteem-enhancing potential of deviant behavior is found in gang membership. Some adolescents who fail to acquire a sense of worth and value through mainstream, pro-social means often seek and achieve a substitute esteem in gangs and antisocial acts.

Hans Toch's (1969) research findings are consistent with Howard Kaplan's data. According to his interviews with violent inmates and parolees, Mr. Toch found that the most common characteristic among them was "self-image compensating" that involved aggression in defense of their self-image, in retribution for aspersions, or to demonstrate that they were worthwhile. Low self-image was at the root of these inmates' need to use aggression.

Violence and Social Responsibility. Testimony presented to the Task Force provided a hypothesis regarding another possible cause of crime and violence. Namely, crime and violence may stem from a diminishing or lack of pro-social values regarding citizenship, honesty, respect for others, and responsibility for one's actions. Such values need to be taught in schools, at home, and in the community at large.

Violence and Mental Health. Low self-esteem is likely to be involved in the complex root causes of both violence and mental illness. However, a common misconception about a link between violence and mental illness needs to be clarified, since a failure to do so might actually promote low self-esteem.

Recent research contradicts the pervasive public fear that the mentally ill, as a group, are more violent than the mentally healthy. In fact, the mentally ill are more likely to be victims of crime than perpetrators.

By its very nature, mental illness damages a person's capacity for interpersonal relationships. In addition, because of their reduced economic base, the mentally ill often reside in less desirable areas, segregated and isolated. The result is separation from routine societal support systems and a consequent damage to their already fragile self-esteem.

Without community mobilization and the development of alternatives to gang activity, our streets will be lost to the violence because law enforcement can*not* do the job alone.

—*Captain Raymond E. Gott, Los Angeles County Sheriff's Department, from a presentation to the Office of Juvenile Justice and Delinquency Prevention, Washington, D.C., September 22, 1989*

Summary on Crime and Violence and Self-esteem

The nature of criminal and juvenile delinquent behavior is so varied and its roots so intertwined with the social, economic, and political order that it is unlikely to be explained by a single theory or alleviated by a single response. Nonetheless, numerous studies and research projects point to self-esteem as a fundamental and critical factor in criminal and violent behavior. Deviant behavior is too often the result of an unstable and unloving home life; alienation from social groups such as school, church, and the community; economic inequities; and cultural and racial discrimination—all crucial to building self-esteem. It may be time for us, as a society, to consider new programs, laws, and policies that recognize the role of self-esteem in the causation of crime and violence. The recommendations that follow are an attempt to move California in that direction.

Key Recommendations on Crime and Violence and Self-esteem

1. Establish a juvenile justice system that will develop personal responsibility in juvenile offenders by imposing consistent and appropriate sanctions for every criminal act.
2. Support the replication of successful community-based juvenile delinquency prevention programs that foster positive self-esteem and personal and social responsibility.

Recommendations on Crime and Violence and Self-esteem in Brief Form

1. Hold juveniles accountable for crime.
2. Replicate programs that foster self-esteem and responsibility.
3. Combat gangs with self-esteem programs in schools.
4. Create community partnerships to develop after-school activities.
5. Establish self-esteem programs in correctional facilities.
6. Develop self-esteem programs for criminal justice agencies.
7. Provide self-management and coping skills for inmates.
8. Promote arts programs in institutional settings.
9. Establish community correctional facilities.

Recommendations, Discussion, and Program Examples on Crime and Violence and Self-esteem

RECOMMENDATION 1

Hold juveniles accountable for crime.

Establish a juvenile justice system that will develop personal responsibility in juvenile offenders by imposing consistent and appropriate sanctions for every criminal act.

For nearly 100 years the juvenile justice system has functioned as a protective nonpunitive rehabilitative, noncriminal system. This philosophy rests on the concept of *parens patriae* in which the government assumes the role of parent, providing functions and services that would normally be provided by the young person's parents. But it overlooks the crucial issue of accountability. Without discrediting the appropriate emphasis placed on counseling, diversion, and rehabilitation, we must recognize that the juvenile justice system has neglected the offender's need to accept responsibility for his or her choices and behavior.

Without sanctions for criminal and antisocial behavior, it is next to impossible to hold youthful offenders accountable for their behavior and to develop their sense of personal responsibility. As a result, today's juvenile justice system inadvertently encourages some youthful offenders to continue criminal behavior. When a youthful offender gets arrested for a relatively minor crime, such as petty theft or vandalism, penalties are almost never imposed. The child is counseled, possibly diverted to a community-based agency, or merely sent home to his or her parents. The message that the system gives this youngster is that society is not really serious about expecting people to obey the law, and that very little, if anything, happens when a juvenile breaks the law.

To have a truly effective juvenile justice system, a system that teaches personal and social responsibility, we must attach a reason-

Kids see that the system is a joke, that unfortunately there are no consequences until they are eighteen or so. That is clearly wrong.

—Dr. Stephen Fleisher, Executive Director, San Fernando Valley Child Guidance Clinic State Task Force on Gangs and Drugs, 1989

©1986 Wernher Krutein/PHOTOVAULT

able sanction to every criminal act, regardless of how minor. The sanction does not need to include incarceration; it could involve community service at the direction of the juvenile court, followed by diversion or counseling. This delivers the message that committing a crime is a serious act for which one will be held accountable.

RECOMMENDATION 2

Replicate programs that foster self-esteem and responsibility.

Support the replication of successful community-based juvenile delinquency prevention programs that foster positive self-esteem and personal and social responsibility.

Community programs not only assist in changing the lives of the youth who participate but also offer an opportunity for citizens to become active in responding to those youth and to have a direct effect on reducing crime in their community. Law enforcement alone will not stop the growth of delinquent behavior. Community self-esteem, however, can be a powerful motivator to set the priorities of the community.

Parents, business leaders, law enforcement officials, and religious leaders need to be encouraged to take some control and jointly deliver the message that criminality is not acceptable, that asocial and antisocial behavior will not be tolerated, and that strong collaboration and cooperation exist among these groups. They can make a commitment to assisting youth in breaking the delinquency cycle. This assistance may be in the form of programs that directly address individual delinquency problems or address the broader focus in the community, such as the following.

- **Breakthrough Foundation's Youth at Risk Program** (3509 Fillmore St., San Francisco, CA 94123, [415] 673-0171): This physically rigorous program helps juvenile delinquents take control of their lives. Presented by the nonprofit educational organization, Breakthrough, the Youth at Risk Program gives communities a way to intervene in the problem of juvenile delinquency. The program spans a two-year period within a community and includes three primary components: start-up, during which time community volunteers are trained to organize, fund, and produce the program; a ten-day course for youth and youth agency staff; and a one-year follow-through evaluation. The ten-day course is the program's focal point. It includes lectures and discussions, group demonstrations and learning processes, daily exercise, and a mountaineering ropes course for the participants to experience the need for mutual trust and communication. Youth have numerous opportunities to experience that they make a difference and to realize that they do have an effect on other human beings. They are shown how to see themselves as the authors, not the victims, of their lives. At the end of the course, each participant identifies and makes a commitment to one or more personal and community projects for the follow-through phase of the program.

- **Casa Victoria for Young Girls** (P. O. Box 6244, Whittier, CA 90609 [213] 941-1279): This is a home for girls on probation, especially Latina and Chicana girls. The program works with girls who have become drug addicts, dropouts, prostitutes, and homeless.
- **Latino Ensemble** (P.O. Box 26A 28, Los Angeles, CA 90026 [213] 484- 9005): This is a nonprofit theatrical company dedicated to the advancement of the Latino culture. Presenting theatrical works in both English and Spanish, the program involves youth from the Echo Park area in theatrical workshops as an alternative to delinquency and gang involvement.

RECOMMENDATION 3

Combat gangs with self-esteem programs in schools.

Encourage training for all personnel who work with youth to use self-esteem-based programs in kindergarten through grade twelve to offset gang affiliation.

People join gangs at early ages and for a variety of reasons, including prestige, a sense of belonging, and economic advantages. As one gang member put it in testimony before the Task Force:

> When we began, 31 percent of all fifth graders indicated attitudes in favor of gangs and drugs. At the end of the program, only 7 percent indicated at risk attitudes.
>
> —*Ernie Paculba, Coordinator, Gang Alternative Program, Los Angeles Unified School District State Task Force on Gangs and Drugs, 1989*

I've been into gangs since I was in the fifth grade. I got into a gang for the prestige, for the girls, and all that. Now I'm into it because of the job situation. I'm twenty-one years old, and I've got two little girls to take care of. There aren't any jobs, something I can do for 20 or 30 years and then retire, so I've got to do this. I've got to pick up a gun and sell dope. Sell dope, making $1,500 or $2,000 a week, that takes care of everything: peas, beans, clothes, plus you've got the prestige still. I like it because it's a fear we put into people. Everybody likes to be in the limelight.

While some communities have implemented successful gang-prevention and intervention strategies, such as those listed below, little in-depth research has been conducted about the origins, procedures, activities, and success rates of these efforts. Such research is necessary if we are to create similar programs or augment existing ones. Without it, law enforcement and community organizations have no rationale or support for seeking new funds or augmentations for gang prevention programs.

- **The Community Access Team** (Officer Balizan, 300 W. Winton Ave., Hayward, CA 94544 [415] 784-7013): Sponsored by the Hayward Police Department, the goal of this program is to obtain employment and develop educational programs for 25 youth gang members per year. Participants receive job training and educational counseling to help them develop good work habits. They are also encouraged to participate in community service projects. In corollary function, the team acts as a liaison between youth gangs and the Hayward Police Department, and between the state labor board and the local Chamber of Commerce.

- **GREAT—Gang Resistance Education and Training** (Los Angeles Unified School District, 450 N. Grand Ave., Los Angeles, CA 90012 [213] 625-5300): This pilot program aims at preventing gang membership and involvement, with a focus on the elementary school level. It emphasizes the development of self-esteem, positive leadership, goal setting, and achievement—in addition to ways to enhance communication and create win-win relationships.

- **Los Angeles Theater Works** (681 Venice Blvd., Venice, CA 90291 [213] 827-0808): This program is directed toward youth involved with crime and violence.

- **The Paramount Plan**: Alternative to Gang Membership (c/o Tony Ostos, 16400 Colorado Ave., Paramount, CA 90723, [213] 531-3503, ext. 221): This program stresses disapproval of gang membership while working to eliminate the future gang membership base and to diminish gang influence. Held in neighborhoods identified by the sheriff's office as "under gang influence," community meetings are aimed at parents and pre-teens. Simultaneously, a fifth-grade anti-gang curriculum, introduced in the Paramount Unified School District in 1982, emphasizes constructive activities available in the neighborhood. Anti-gang materials and posters are available to community members on request.

- **Stop Gap Theatre**: (P.O. Box 494, Laguna Beach, CA 92652 [619] 722-7727): This program aims at enhancing the self-esteem of people in all six of the Task Force's "social concerns" categories.

- **Triple Crown Youth Coalition** (103 1/2 South Meadowbrook Dr., San Diego, CA 92114 [619] 267-0777): A work program funded by the City of San Diego, Triple Crown currently employs 25 to 30 local gang members. The program stresses self-esteem, the value of work, and good work habits. Business people and community members become actively involved with eradicating gangs by developing a rapport with neighborhood youth, gaining their respect, and working with them to find alternatives to gang activity, particularly through employment. Anti-gang prevention programs need to focus on young children who are not yet involved in gangs. Programs for older youth should contain a work component.

RECOMMENDATION 4

Create community partnerships to develop after-school activities.

Create a public/private partnership to encourage and assist after-school youth groups that promote self-esteem and personal and social responsibility.

Given research indicating that, without healthy alternatives, youth seek negative and antisocial ways to bolster their self-esteem, the need for programs that provide constructive and pro-social experiences becomes critical.

After-school activities and clubs based on student interests have nearly disappeared in many of our communities and public schools. With many parents both working, few adults are available as leaders. In addition, many teachers and students commute long distances to school and are less inclined to stay after classes.

We need to develop support structures and positive peer groups among our youth. For example, South Central Los Angeles maintained a demonstration project for three years that included full-time clinical social workers and family counselors. The organizers discovered that many black inner-city churches had auditoriums and classrooms that went unused during the week. So that the youth would not be on the street, these organizers had activities going on from mid-afternoon until late at night.

- **Urban Youth Lock-In: Gang and Drug Prevention for At-Risk Youth** (Dr. Ralph Dawson, Director of the Center for the Study of Black on Black Crime, Student Health Center, CSULA, 5151 State University Dr., Los Angeles, CA 90032 [213] 343-3331): Utilizing community church facilities, this project provides a broad-based early intervention program for at-risk youth. It centers around a 24-hour urban retreat during which the youth meet with community professionals, church people, and select role models. Approximately 4,500 at-risk youth in six major urban centers—San Diego, Los Angeles, Fresno, San Francisco, Oakland, and Sacramento—will be served. Out-of-state contacts are being made. Follow-up mentor-youth meetings with the youth, project staff, and volunteers will reinforce the commitments made by the youth to remain drug and gang free for at least 90 days.

RECOMMENDATION 5

Establish self-esteem programs in correctional facilities.

Encourage all county and state correctional facilities to work with other organizations to establish programs that enhance self-esteem. Objectives include basic skills, character development, and educational, vocational, and social training. All such programs need to be evaluated for effectiveness.

This section discusses issues and programs for both juveniles and adults.

Juvenile Facilities

According to a 1988 study, California has some of the toughest youth sentencing policies and overcrowded youth institutions in the nation. An increasing number of California's youth are being incarcerated and for longer periods of time.

A concurrent opinion poll demonstrated overwhelming support of a separate juvenile justice system with rehabilitation as its primary goal. Californians also showed a preference for public spending on programs to educate and train youthful offenders to become law-abiding citizens. As Joe Sandoval, Secretary of Corrections, stated in his testimony before the Task Force, wards unfortunately suffer from a lack of both self-esteem and social responsibility. As he concluded, therefore, "Efforts to improve self-esteem are crucial in the correctional setting."

If these youth are ever to gain a sense of worth and become productive citizens of the state, we must provide them with knowledge and practical life skills that will assist them in gaining employment on release and coping with problems that brought them into the institution originally.

- **Free Venture Program**, California Youth Authority (Fred Mills, 4241 Williamsborough Dr., Suite 227, Sacramento, CA 95823 [916] 427-6674): This program was created in 1985 by a task force representing private industry, labor, county government, the Youth and Adult Correctional Agency, and the Youth Authority. In a partnership between government and businesses, wards are employed by private-sector firms. The program enhances the self-esteem of these offenders by enabling them to prove themselves in a real-world setting. Each ward must put 40 percent of monies earned into a savings account. They also pay taxes, so they see themselves as contributing members of society. Developing a work ethic for themselves encourages feelings of accomplishment and self-worth. Finally, each participant develops a work history and job reference which increases self-worth and contributes to the probability of parole success. Of the program's 40 graduates, only two have fallen back into the system, and both of these were out at least a year before their return.

- **Senior Tutors for Youth in Detention** (Sondra Napell, 3640 Grand Ave., Suite 5, Oakland, CA 94610 [415] 839-1039): Boys in San Francisco's Youth Guidance Center are tutored weekly by retirees from the Rossmoor retirement community in Walnut Creek. The tutors provide two hours in written and verbal skills, vocational opportunities, mock interviews, parenting skills, and ethics and morality. Begun in 1983, the program provides boys with positive learning experiences and consistent caring and encouragement from adults.

Adult Facilities

Meaningful educational and vocational programs within our adult correctional facilities can provide inmates with goals, build self-esteem, foster pride in learning a skill or advancing academically, and teach pro-social values and responsibility.

Current programs such as the Conservation Camps, Community Crews, and Prison Industries enable prisoners to participate in activities such as fire fighting, forest land management, road repair, flood control, and building maintenance, as well as a variety of manufacturing, agricultural, and service enterprises. Such programs enable prisoners to learn important job skills and thereby enhance their self-esteem and confidence. Programs can be designed so that moneys earned can provide restitution and compensation to victims of crime and also pay a portion of the costs of criminals' incarceration.

- **Bread and Roses** (78 Throckmorton, Mill Valley, CA 94941-1994 [415] 381-0320): In this program drama is performed for prisoners.

- **Breaking Barriers Program** (Department of Corrections, P.O. Box 942883, Sacramento, CA 94283-0001 [916] 445-5691): A six-month pilot project at the California Medical Facility-South, Facility IV, exposed a maximum of 1,200 inmates to the self-esteem principles advocated by the Pacific Institute of Seattle. It focused on overcoming internal personal barriers to success. Components include improving self-image, changing habits and attitudes, increasing self-awareness, building self-confidence, and increasing social responsibility. Part of the mandatory 30-hour, five-day orientation program for newly arrived inmates, this 15-hour program can provide prisoners with the knowledge and incentive to map out a plan of action for their incarceration. This also enables their successful transition back to the community. Current inmates are allowed to participate.

- **Correctional Education** (Hall of Justice, 211, W. Temple St., Los Angeles, CA 90012 [213] 974-5096): The Los Angeles County Sheriff's Department and the Hacienda/La Puente Unified School District are committed to policy of supporting inmates' reentry into a more positive role in society. They provide an accredited program of academic and vocational education for the 23,000 persons incarcerated in the custodial facilities of Los Angeles County.

- **Glendale Humanistic Psychological Center** (416 East Broadway Ave., Suite 115, Glendale, CA 91205 [818] 500-9835): This program is designed for Hispanic sex offenders who are on probation after being released from prison. The Center communicates acceptance, empathy, warmth, understanding toward clients, with educational and therapeutic approaches for building self-esteem, taking personal and social responsibility, becoming more assertive, and learning communication skills in human relations. Emphasis is placed on the process of change within the individual and on cross-cultural issues.

- **Voices** (Deuel Vocational Institution, P.O. Box 400, Tracy, CA 95376 [209] 466-8055): A six-week inmate-education and parole-based support/monitoring program, Voices is directed toward reducing violent responses to stress. Through classroom education and subsequent behavioral support of selected inmates and their families, the program seeks to sensitize inmates to the short- and long-range effects of their criminal behavior on victims, to reduce the future incidence of their violent behavior, and to increase their ability to meet personal and social responsibilities. Components include communication skills, information about crimes against persons, family and life and gender roles, and child-rearing skills.

RECOMMENDATION 6

Develop self-esteem programs for criminal justice agencies.

Create policies and practices within our criminal justice agencies that promote self-esteem and both the physical and social well-being of staff members and offenders, and also raise the level of respect accorded to both groups.

The level of self-esteem among criminal justice staff and offenders is often critical not only in crises but also in day-to-day operations. Personnel and operational policies that specifically seek to upgrade self-esteem may alleviate tension, improve service, and help rehabilitate clients. This requires institutional policies to be sensitive to issues of pride and shame. Agencies must examine policies regulating the activities of clients and wards, work to eliminate unnecessary rules, encourage an atmosphere of mutual respect, train staff to be sensitive

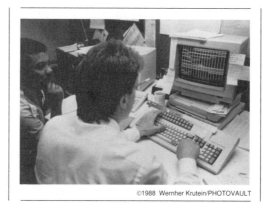

©1988 Wernher Krutein/PHOTOVAULT

to shame and the offender's intense need for respectful treatment, and train offenders to interact with staff in respectful, productive ways.

Whenever policies change, it is critical that staff are explicitly brought into the planning process and provided with educational programs. People in positions of authority within the criminal justice system need to understand and be sensitive to the principles of self-esteem and the relationships between pride and shame, respectful treatment, and crime and violence. This training needs to include not only the staff of agencies, such as prisons, mental hospitals, and welfare agencies, but also judges, probation officers, and law enforcement personnel.

Within these programs, people need to become aware that respect and disrespect are conveyed less by what is said than by how it is said. Respect is signaled much more by facial expression, bearing, and intonation than by specific words. Clients who are already in a disadvantaged position are acutely sensitive to insulting or demeaning mannerisms, no matter how subtle or unintended. Becoming aware of the importance of this often makes it easier for a staff member to discuss a client's conduct or concerns without alienating or embarrassing either party. It enables cooperation and helps increase self-esteem.

RECOMMENDATION 7

Provide self-management and coping skills for inmates.

Provide inmates with the opportunity for self-esteem education in self-management, stress reduction, and relaxation techniques that relieve anger, anxiety, and fear.

If prisoners can learn to alleviate their own psychological stress and replace it with a peaceful state of mind, then they may be less likely to victimize themselves or others. They may also succeed in attempts to live pro-socially and productively. In fact, research with San Quentin inmates indicates that offenders trained in meditation and relaxation techniques evidence lower recidivism rates than those who are not.

One aspect of stress reduction and self-management is the acquisition of skills for survival in society. The greater the degree of skill acquisition, the greater probability that those coping skills may reduce stress.

- **How to Be Successful** (Thomas Jefferson Center, 202 S. Lake Ave., Pasadena, CA 91104 [818] 792-8130): The program has reduced violence in the San Diego Juvenile Hall. It focuses on specific skill development related to personal and social responsibility, self-esteem enhancement, and stress reduction. The program teaches elemental skills such as being on time, being prepared, and being a goal setter. It also teaches skills such as ethical decision making, a process of thinking called STAR (stop, think, act, and review), and empathy.

RECOMMENDATION 8

Promote arts programs in institutional settings.

Support programs in the creative arts that promote the development of self-esteem and personal and social responsibility for individuals who are incarcerated or at risk thereof.

The learning and practice of art requires patience, commitment, self-discipline, imagination, and an attitude of cooperation. To master an arts discipline, one grows in self-confidence and acquires a feeling of competence. These attributes make programs in the visual, literary, and performing arts particularly effective for incarcerated individuals.

By acquiring artistic skills, participants learn to affect their environment in a constructive manner. For some, learning a creative process also produces a fundamental change in attitude about themselves and others. Research conducted by the California Department of Corrections and the Law Enforcement Assistance Administration indicates that inmates involved in ongoing arts programs show a 70 to 80 percent reduction in violent and other disruptive behavior while in prison and are 40 percent less likely to return to prison once released.

• **Arts in Corrections** (Department of Corrections, 1515 S. Street, Sacramento, CA 95814 [916] 323-3791): The goal of this highly regarded program is to "improve the prison experience by providing participants an opportunity to affect their own environment and begin changing their attitudes about themselves and others." Begun in 1977 at the California Medical Facility at Vacaville, the program serves each of California's 18 correctional facilities and is the largest institutional arts program in the world.

The program is based on the belief that an inmate can improve his or her self-esteem and, thus, behavior by replacing lost physical freedom with an inner freedom gained through the discipline and rewards of art. The program provides an opportunity for inmates to learn, experience, and be rewarded for individual responsibility and self-discipline. Involvement can lead to an increase in constructive self-sufficiency, heightened self-esteem, and reduced tension. The 1987 Arts-in-Corrections recidivism study showed that participants' rate of return was reduced by 51 percent.

RECOMMENDATION 9

Establish community correctional facilities.

Contribute to the self-esteem of inmates and staff by encouraging correctional agencies to establish decentralized correctional facilities within or near their community of residence.

The centralization and relative isolation of youth correctional facilities from their respective communities affects the level of self-esteem of both inmates and staff. As long as staff and inmates are separated from their communities of origin, those communities can disown them emotionally, treating them as aliens and reducing their social status. This directly contradicts any effort to increase the social standing of the staff by means of changes in institutional policy and continuing education.

The California Task Force on the Mentally Ill is preparing a proposal that calls for the decentralization of the mental health system. The proposal requests that treatment units be small enough to be located in or near the community from which their staff and clients are drawn. The same reasoning applies to the correctional system. The initial investment would be more than repaid in the increases in the efficiency and humaneness of the new programs.

References for Crime and Violence and Self-esteem

"Crime and Delinquency in California, 1988." Sacramento, Calif.: Bureau of Criminal Statistics, Office of the Attorney General, Department of Justice, 1989.

Dollard, J., L. Doob, N. Miller, O. Mowrer, and R. Sears. *Frustration and Aggression*. New Haven, Conn.: Yale University Press, 1939.

Epstein, S., and S. P. Taylor. "Instigation to Aggression as a Function of Degree of Defeat and Perceived Aggressive Intent of the Opponent," *Journal of Personality*, Vol. 35 (1967), 265–289.

Feshbach, Seymour. "The Dynamics and Morality of Violence and Aggression," *American Psychologist*, Vol. 26 (1971,) 281–292.

Green, R. G. "Effects of Frustration, Attack, and Prior Training in Aggression upon Aggressive Behavior," *Journal of Personality and Social Psychology*, Vol. 9 (1968), 316–321.

Kaplan, Howard B. *Self-Attitudes and Deviant Behavior*. Pacific Palisades, Calif.: Goodyear, 1975.

Kaplan, Howard B. *Deviant Behavior in Defense of Self*. New York: Academic Press, 1980.

Lally, Ronald J., P. L. Mangione, and A. S. Honig. "Long Range Impact of an Early Intervention with Low-Income Children and Their Families," *The Syracuse University Family Development Research Program*. San Francisco: Far West Laboratory, 1987.

Toch, Hans *Violent Man*. Chicago: Aldine, 1969.

McCord, W., J. McCord, and A. Howard. "Familial Correlations of Aggression in Nondeliquent Male Children," *Journal of Abnormal and Social Psychology*, Vol. 62 (1961), 79–93.

Monahan, J., and H. J. Steadman, "Crime and Mental Disorder: an Epidemiological Approach," in *Crime and Justice: An Annual Review of Research*, Vol IV. Chicago: University of Chicago Press, 1983.

"Report to Attorney General John K. Van de Kamp on Patrick Edward Purdy in the Cleveland School Killings." Sacramento, Calif.: Office of the Attorney General, Oct., 1989.

Scheff, Thomas J., Suzanne M. Retzinger, and Michael T. Ryan. "Crime, Violence, and Self-Esteem: Review and Proposals," in *The Social Importance of Self-esteem*. Berkeley, Calif.: University of California Press, 1989.

Poverty, Chronic Welfare Dependency, and Self-esteem

*O*f all the social concerns examined by the Task Force, the correlation between chronic welfare dependency and self-esteem was the one most difficult to isolate and define. When we examine poor academic achievement or the propensity for criminal behavior, for example, low self-esteem has an evident correlation, as well as being a resulting condition. This connecting link is far more tenuous, however, concerning welfare recipients. While there is considerable evidence that being on welfare in our society can eat away at a person's sense of worth, it is not so clear that low self-esteem leads to welfare dependency.

Total federal and state expenditures on "social welfare" in California in 1988 were $22 billion—nearly 36 percent of the entire state budget (Governor's Budget Act, Chapter 313, Statutes of 1988). Of that amount, only 7.3 percent went to Aid to Families with Dependent Children (AFDC), the one program most commonly referred to as *welfare*. This tiny fraction receives the lion's share of political and media attention, however. Other programs funded out of the welfare budget include: Supplemental Security Income (SSI), In-Home Supportive Service (IHSS), disability and unemployment insurance, mental health services, foster care, Medi-Cal, and alcohol and drug programs. The great discrepancy between public perceptions and the facts reflects the depth and ambivalence of public feelings about welfare and the people who receive it.

Americans traditionally affirm their feelings of compassion for those who are in need, and AFDC clearly qualifies as an example. AFDC payments are instituted by the Legislature to relieve the poverty of families in dire need. On the other hand, many Americans express equally strong emotions about those who "live on the public dole" and "fail to carry their share of the load." Understandably, most taxpayers resent having to give from their hard-earned wages for the support of people they perceive to be not working and choosing not to do so. For most of us, these two conflicting emotions remain unresolved.

The Task Force recognizes that a sense of being able to care for one's self and one's family is an important component of self-esteem. It is also true that self-esteem based solely on external achievements and success leads not to emotional stability, but to anxiety, competitiveness, and self-doubt. Healthy self-esteem arises from a deep inner sense of personal worth, a confidence that allows a person to continue to function and make responsible choices in spite of pain, failure, and loss.

Though self-esteem is ultimately a decision each person makes for himself or herself, a positive choice is greatly enhanced by an accepting, affirming, and encouraging environment. People who are reared, or are forced to live, in the midst of ridicule, rejection, and demeaning behavior find it very difficult to choose a positive self-image.

In the same way, people living in circumstances of material deprivation and limited economic opportunity are not likely to be favorably conditioned toward feelings of high self-esteem. As one Humboldt county resident expressed to the Task Force at its public hearing, "Many of the problems associated with [low] self-esteem, from children to elderly adults, are a direct result of the effect of poverty in our community. It's important to recognize that there is an interaction between social problems and self-esteem. It's difficult to think about esteem when you're struggling for survival." Low self-esteem, hopelessness, and alienation are often the concomitants of poverty and economic want for both child and parent. Economic well-being and the financial and psychological rewards of work, on the other hand, make it easier to form the essential foundation for healthy child development.

The following sections discuss several issues relating to self-esteem, and personal and social responsibility, poverty, welfare dependency, child care, and working parents.

It is not easy for men to rise whose qualities are thwarted by poverty.

—*Juvenal*

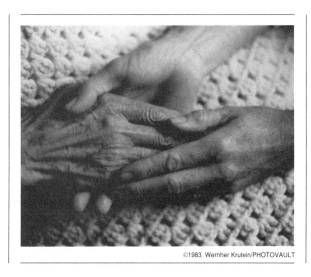

©1983 Wernher Krutein/PHOTOVAULT

The Effects of Poverty

After parental care, economic status is the most consistent predictor of a child's well-being in terms of health, academic achievement, and emotions. *Today one out of every five children in California lives in a family whose income is below the federally defined poverty level (currently $12,100 for a family of four). Many more children live just above the poverty line.* Since 1981, the proportion of children living in California has increased substantially, as has the disparity between the poorest children and all others. As a group, children are worse off economically than are adults.

The general well-being of a child is affected in both absolute and relative terms. Living in poverty greatly diminishes a child's access to adequate food, health care, clothing, and shelter. Perhaps more to the point of the Task Force's work is the child's relative economic status. Numerous studies have determined that the family's economic status is the single most powerful predictor of a child's opportunity for success and self-sufficiency in adulthood. According to a recent study of the Center for Policy Analysis of California Education (PACE), a joint project of the University of California at Berkeley and Stanford University:

> *A family's economic status often determines the quality of the neighborhood in which the child lives; the child's access to services such as libraries, parks, and youth organizations; the availability of complete medical care; and many other important resources. In addition, relative deprivation can negatively affect aspirations and self-concept.*

In her book, *Within Our Reach: Breaking the Cycle of Disadvantage and Despair*, Lisbeth B. Schorr reports that in the past moving out of poverty did not require school success; but jobs that allowed this kind of upward mobility no longer exist. The average annual income of high school dropouts increased by 18 percent between 1959 and 1973, but decreased by 37 percent between 1973 and 1986. This trend has reversed and, in fact, doubled. High school dropouts today, Schorr reported, are three times as likely to be arrested, twice as likely to be unemployed, and six times more likely to be unwed parents.

"The notion that in the world of social programs, nothing works," Lisbeth Schorr stated, "is a . . . myth." School-based health clinics reduce rates of teen pregnancy; comprehensive prenatal services reduce rates of low birth-weight babies; intensive family support leads to fewer children removed from their homes, less child abuse, and less welfare dependency; and high quality preschool education has long-term effects on children, resulting in less future delinquency and unemployment. "Not only do we know that [social programs] work, we also know how and why they work," said Schorr.

These are the characteristics of successful intervention programs:

- They are comprehensive and intensive. They provide a wide variety of services, are flexible, are provided in nontraditional set-

Unfortunately, many Americans live on the outskirts of hope—some because of their poverty, some because of their color, and all too many because of both. Our task is to help replace their despair with opportunity.

—Lyndon Baines Johnson

tings, at nontraditional hours, and they treat the whole person or family as they are.

- Successful programs deal with the child as a part of the family and the family as part of the neighborhood. They are supportive of and collaborative with parents, and they take into account the real world of the people they serve.
- Program staff have the time, training, and skills to build relationships of trust and respect with children and their families. They allow children and their families to gain greater control of their lives. How services are provided is as important as what services are provided.

Chronic Welfare Dependency and Self-esteem

Slow rises worth, by poverty depressed.

—*Samuel Johnson*

Women heads of households are caught in the middle of society's ambivalence toward welfare. In an era when more than half of the married mothers work outside the home for at least part of the day, there is a growing expectation that single heads of households should work as well. Certainly, given the relationship among work, self-sufficiency, and self-esteem, all mothers should have the opportunity for gainful employment, along with the transportation services that would make the workplace accessible and the quality of child care that would help ensure their children's healthy development.

As it exists today, though, the AFDC program tends to penalize or de-motivate mothers who work. The program drastically reduces benefits as earnings increase, leaving those who do work no better off, and perhaps in worse condition (with no medical benefits or child care allowance, for example) than those who remain dependent on AFDC.

A study by D. T. Ellwood in 1986 noted that only one woman in five who left welfare did so as a result of increased income from earnings, and that earnings sufficient to achieve self-support required full-year, full-time work at approximately 2,000 hours annually. Complete self-sufficiency through earnings for single-parent households with small children may not be a realistic policy goal for AFDC recipients. However, the option, if not the mandate, for gainful employment of some extent should be made available, along with the support services necessary to make the choices realistic and likely to result in success.

Several studies point to changes in family or household composition, rather than changes in income level, as the primary cause for accepting welfare benefits. A 1983 study of the reasons for going on welfare found that "three-fourths of all spells on AFDC begin with a relationship change whereby a female headed family is created. Only 12 percent of beginnings can be traced to earnings decreases." (Bane and Ellwood, 1983).

In his review of the literature on behalf of the Task Force, Leonard Schneiderman, Dean of the School of Social Welfare, University of California, Los Angeles, found that "becoming a wife is the primary reason that women leave welfare" and that "earnings gains account for only 21 percent of all exits."

The probability of remaining on welfare over a period of six years is related to the following variables: market productivity, the number of children, educational level, teenager at first birth, attitudinal factors, and welfare grants. Dean Schneiderman found that over 40 percent of those who ever receive AFDC receive it for no more than four years. Yet nearly 25 percent eventually use AFDC again in ten or more years. Occasional AFDC receipt is common; persistent welfare receipt is not. "Movement on and off welfare rolls is widespread." (Duncan and Hoffman, 1987)

One major research effort evaluated the *stigma* argument, namely, that welfare recipients "incorporate the general negative views of themselves held by others, thus reducing feelings of self-worth" (Nichols-Casebolt, 1986). This study revealed that welfare is associated with a decrease in the psychological well-being of the recipient.

While inconclusive, the evidence implicating chronic welfare dependency with some deterioration in self-esteem is stronger than the evidence linking it with a prior self-esteem condition. It is easy to see how chronic material deprivation below the poverty line, coupled with external controls associated with welfare, can have psychological consequences. T. J. Kane (1987) theorizes that the victimization and loss of control associated with chronic poverty may breed dysfunctional psychological coping mechanisms such as learned helplessness.

The poor, in general, and many welfare recipients, in particular, also experience nonresponsive bureaucratic environments over which they have no control. After some time, even when a situation arises in which they could assert control, they often do not. Learned helplessness may thus prevent welfare recipients and the poor from recognizing new opportunities. By implication, structural changes alone may not be sufficient to move individuals who are chronically dependent on welfare to a state of independence.

Child Care and Working Parents

According to a publication of the Child Care Action Campaign, only 7 percent of all American households fit the picture of the "traditional" American family: mother at home caring for the family and father in the work force ("Investing in Our Children," 1985). Over 60 percent of all families have two or more wage earners, and 54 percent of all women are in the paid work force. These statistics suggest the necessity of certain changes in the workplace. The U.S. Department of Labor reports that there are over 20 million families in the United States that have children age thirteen years or younger. These families are most likely to require child care.

Renewed public interest in early childhood programs in the United States springs both from the growing need for child care and from the need to lessen the harmful consequences of childhood poverty. A case in point is the High/Scope Foundation's Perry Preschool study which strikingly demonstrates the potential benefits of high-quality early childhood programs for poor children (Berrrueta-Clement, et al., 1984). In the study, poor three- and four-year-olds were randomly assigned either to a group that attended the Perry Preschool Program or to a group that did not. Follow-up on both groups years later showed that preschool participation had apparently increased the percentages of persons who, at age nineteen, were literate, employed, and enrolled in postsecondary education. It had also reduced the percentages who were school dropouts, labeled mentally retarded, or on welfare.

An economic cost-benefit analysis of the Perry Preschool Program and its long-term effects revealed that such a program can be an excellent investment for taxpayers, returning $6 for every dollar invested in a one-year program, and $3 more for every dollar invested in a two-year program.

Other research on good early childhood programs for poor children confirms that such programs have positive short-, mid-, and long-term results. These programs help children's intellectual and social performance as they begin school, probably help children achieve greater school success, and can help young people achieve greater socioeconomic success and social responsibility. Yet, despite these findings, fewer than one in three poor children have the opportunity to attend a preschool program.

These findings apply to children who live in poverty and are at risk of school failure. There is less evidence on preschool program effectiveness for children who are not poor or otherwise at risk of school failure. A good supposition is that a preschool effect found for poor children would also apply to middle-class children, but to a lesser extent.

Impressive results were achieved only by good preschool programs. These are characterized by the following: developmentally appropriate curriculum and assessment procedures, teaching teams that are trained in early childhood development and continue to receive such training, and administrative support that includes curricular leadership. Classes have two adults and fewer than 20 children, and systematic efforts involve parents as partners in their children's preschool. Programs such as these yield a high return on investment, and they make more economic sense than poor inexpensive programs with a low return.

It would be hard to imagine that society could find a higher yield for a dollar of investment than that found in preschool programs for its at-risk children.

Investing in Our Children (1985)

Summary to Welfare and Self-esteem

The economic context that encircles families and individuals powerfully influences not only their material quality of life but also their spiritual and emotional well-being. Many problems are associated with dissatisfaction over work, or the lack of it. In less severe cases, problems involve relieving the stress related to job dissatisfaction and unpleasant working conditions. In extreme cases, the stress of poverty breeds ignorance, rage, and helplessness—and with them comes their inevitable effect: low self-esteem.

With the following recommendations, the Task Force seeks to recognize the changes in family composition and to promote economic and workplace conditions that enable single parents as well as intact families at risk to establish nurturing home environments that encourage pro-social character development and healthy self-esteem.

Key Recommendations on Welfare and Self-esteem

1. Support and implement programs that assist long-term welfare recipients to grow in self-esteem and responsibility so they can move from the welfare rolls to independence.
2. Encourage aid and assistance programs such as AFDC to enable single parents to establish nurturing home environments by providing optional services, such as training for effective child rearing, independent living skills, educational and vocational counseling, and child-care options.

Recommendations on Welfare in Brief Form

1. Support programs that assist long-term welfare recipients toward independence.
2. Encourage programs that provide parents with the tools to be good parents.
3. Encourage programs that establish peer support groups.
4. Provide in-service self-esteem training to staff who work with welfare recipients.
5. Implement welfare reform programs that alter attitudes and enhance motivation.
6. Provide incentives for communities and businesses to work together to promote youth programs.

Recommendations, Discussion, and Program Examples on Welfare and Self-esteem

RECOMMENDATION 1

Support programs that assist long-term welfare recipients toward independence.

Support and implement programs that assist long-term welfare recipients to grow in self-esteem and responsibility so they can move from the welfare rolls to independence.

The repetition of welfare dependency between generations is a topic of considerable fiscal and policy interest. Some observers of poverty and welfare see a condition of "learned helplessness" as a characteristic transmitted from parents to children. Through early socialization, parental failures can be passed on to children in the form of low self-esteem, weak character development, and a "doomed to fail" attitude.

To break this vicious cycle, we need to make it possible for welfare recipients to secure employment that provides sufficient earnings to pay for child care, medical insurance, and other basic necessities. Through early health care, childhood education, and nutritious food, we can help ensure that every child in California gets the right start.

The AFDC program needs to consider policy and program changes that would continue to provide supplemental care income, food stamps, and child care until the head of household achieves sufficient earnings to provide those basic necessities. If they could be assured of basic benefits for their children, many more welfare recipients would be working today and providing a more positive role model for their children, thereby nurturing character development and personal responsibility.

©1986 Wernher Krutein/PHOTOVAULT

- **Indian Health Program** (Rural and Community Health Division, 714 P Street, Room 576, Sacramento, CA 95814 [916] 323-7433): This program provides financial and technical assistance to California clinics that provide Native American Indians with primary medical and dental care. This program strongly advocates Community Health Representatives (CHR) and encourages Indians to become a vital part of their health care delivery systems. The CHR program provides jobs and promotional opportunities for Indians in communities with high unemployment.

- **The Job Club.** Many people working with GAIN participants believe that self-esteem may contribute more to successful employment than specific job skills and work experience. Self-esteem building is most apparent during that portion of the program called *Job Club*. Job Clubs are intensive three-week efforts during which GAIN participants first learn the basics of job hunting and then put those skills to work by actively seeking employment. While Job Clubs are effective in teaching job skills, their lasting benefits derive from their ability to raise self-esteem and motivate participants.

RECOMMENDATION 2

Encourage programs that provide parents with the tools to be good parents.

Encourage aid and assistance programs, such as AFDC, to enable parents to establish nurturing home environments by providing optional services, such as training for effective parenting, independent living skills, educational and vocational counseling, and child-care options.

The AFDC program must be encouraged to develop or collaborate with support programs designed to meet the unique needs of single parents with young children. This reaffirms the profound and primary role a parent plays in developing positive self-esteem and social responsibility in his or her children.

Families headed by single women are the poorest of all major demographic groups in the United States, regardless of how poverty is measured. Their economic position relative to that of other groups, such as the aged and the disabled, has declined steadily during the past two decades. Most working single mothers do not receive child support from the fathers, and they earn wages lower than those of other women. Their wages generally are not high enough to raise them and their children above the poverty level.

A single mother with small children must play two roles: breadwinner and nurturer. But she cannot simultaneously work at a paying job and be at home with her children to love and care for them and to participate in their education. We must therefore balance our support for employing welfare recipients with the broader social goal of creating stable, loving homes in which children can develop self-esteem and learn to grow into caring, responsible adults. We must develop programs that recognize life stages and allow options, including full-time and part-time employment, supplemental benefits, graduated financial support for mothers, and adequate day care during the critical first five years of the child's life.

A longitudinal experiment conducted by Syracuse University's Family Development Research Program (Lally, et al., 1987) underscores the parent's importance in child development. The program was an effort "to improve the 'well-being' of these children born into environments sparse in the benefits that money, education, and job status can bring." Of the 108 families chosen for this study, 85 percent were single-head-of-household families. According to the report of the experiment:

> *The major premise of the FDRP was that parents are the primary teachers and sustaining caregiving persons in a young child's life. Affective and interpersonal relations with the parent would have a profound impact on the learning motivation and competence of the developing infant. Thus, the major thrust of the intervention program was to maximize family functioning.*

The long-term results were exceptional. Measured in terms of the cost to law enforcement agencies, the problems encountered by the young people in the untreated control group were ten times those in the program group.

- **Project Self-Reliance** (150 West Cerritos, Building #4, Anaheim, CA 92805 [714] 772-8285). An independent living center, this program works to increase the self-esteem of the disabled population by providing assertiveness training to enable clients to seek employment, housing, and transportation and to manage their personal finances. The clients' increased sense of control over the direction of their own lives helps build a foundation for future achievements.

RECOMMENDATION 3

Encourage programs that establish peer support groups.

Encourage aid and assistance programs to help establish peer support groups that foster learning, self-confidence, and motivation.

GAIN, California's version of the national JOBS work-welfare legislation, mandates that all welfare recipients with children above age three engage in an education, job-training, and job-search program. Because most people on welfare have not traditionally excelled in education and employment, and because self-confidence is requisite to success in these areas, self-esteem is a key issue for GAIN administrators.

Fortunately, GAIN's program and funding structure allows for support groups in which self-esteem and personal social responsibility can be nurtured. Some counties, such as Napa and Los Angeles, have developed model program components: job search, work experience, education, and training. These can be provided in other counties by the local welfare department or another community organization.

Support groups need to be facilitated by empathetic staff who understand the special barriers welfare recipients face in job searches. Support groups within GAIN provide the mechanism to make participants' hope a reality.

- **GAIN** (Policy Implementation Bureau, Department of Social Services, 744 P Street, Sacramento, CA 95814. Contact should be made with the local County Welfare Department): California's welfare reform program recognizes the important role self-esteem plays in gaining independence through employment. This program offers a comprehensive range of support services, including job search, basic adult education, courses in English as a second language, career assessment, vocational education, on-the-job training, transitional employment, child care, and transportation. A central directive mandates all participants to be enrolled in school, job training, or job-search activities.

- **The GOALS Program** (Foundation for Self-Esteem, 6035 Bristol Parkway, Culver City, CA 90230 [213] 568-1505): A component of the GAIN program, GOALS is a multimedia self-esteem building and motivational training program. Developed by the Foundation for Self-Esteem, the program builds self-esteem, self-sufficiency skills, and motivation in people on welfare. This helps them to become eligible for, to seek, and to retain meaningful employment. The program features a three-and-one-half-hour video program, a participant "Guidebook to Personal Success," and a one-hour audiocassette, "GOALS: Guide to Personal Success." Welfare recipients participate in a two-day training program. Follow-up activities are outlined in the facilitator's manual. In the fall of 1990, this program will be available in several languages.

RECOMMENDATION 4

Provide in-service self-esteem training to staff who work with welfare recipients.

The dignity of welfare recipients should be addressed by providing in-service self-esteem awareness training to staff who work with them.

On the one hand, there's a long standing stereotype concerning the impersonal and insensitive treatment of welfare recipients at the hands of uncaring and disgruntled welfare workers. On the other hand, many eligibility workers are caught between the watchful eye of policymakers and the AFDC recipients in dire need of services. This dilemma is further complicated by the rapidly changing demographics of California's population, which intensifies the need for increased cultural awareness and second language capabilities. There is a crucial need for training and procedures which recognize the dignity and worth of both recipients and staff.

Several California counties have begun to recognize the need to acknowledge the important public service provided by eligibility workers, and these counties have acted to maintain a supportive environment to foster a greater sense of meaning in their work.

- **National Eligibility Worker Association** (Brenda Crawford, President, Box 1616, Beckley, WV 25802-1615 [304] 348-8290): This group is designed to promote the professional status of eligibility workers, with the ultimate goal of enhancing the worker-client relationship. The group focuses on the distinct role of eligibility workers.

- **Professional Respect Integrity Dedication Excellence (PRIDE)** (Mendocino County Department of Social Services, Dennis R. Denny, Courthouse, Ukiah, CA 95482 [707] 463-4588): This program establishes a set of personal goals and provides training and encouragement to motivate social workers to act courteously and professionally, to take pride in their work, and to deal with relational problems/conflicts in a positive way. The program also gives the workers recognition for their efforts and reinforces attitudes that allow individuals to learn from mistakes in a constructive manner.

RECOMMENDATION 5

Implement welfare reform programs that alter attitudes and enhance motivation.

Request the Department of Social Services to implement welfare reform programs that include provisions for programs that motivate and promote self-sufficiency, self-esteem, and personal and social responsibility.

Much of the current debate about welfare reform has focused changing the mix of income available to poor families from employment, family support, and income transfers. However, the AFDC program reduced the child poverty rate by just 4 percent in 1985, and the average length of dependence on AFDC benefits is almost seven years. The AFDC program has essentially operated as a cash payment program that does little to assist recipients in overcoming barriers to self-sufficiency, such as language deficiencies, absence of job skills, child care needs, and poor health. It also does little to relieve child poverty. In addition, research suggests that long-term welfare receipt may undermine the individual's perceived capacity to exercise control over events in his or her personal life. Public policy has fallen short of its goal, and changes should bring poor children and their families above the poverty level while encouraging self-sufficiency.

With child care, education, training, job placement, and counseling, some welfare recipients can increase their income from employment. Work training programs may include motivational and psychological components designed to alter attitudes and enhance client motivation, but these services must not substitute for new and expanded transition opportunities. To reduce welfare dependency and poverty, we need to enable the family's earnings (or a combination of earnings and public benefits) to rise above the poverty level.

Workfare programs that increase income from salaries and wages probably have their greatest effect on an individual's self-esteem and motivation. Attention should be given to creating workplaces respectful of working welfare recipients and mindful of their needs for special support and training without reinforcing or inducing values and habits that encourage prolonged dependency. In addition, education, training, improved health care, and social services offered as part of these programs could provide care-giving parents and children with long-term benefits that are not work specific.

RECOMMENDATION 6

Provide incentives for communities and businesses to work together to promote youth programs.

Provide economic incentives for private-sector organizations and communities to promote self-esteem by establishing jointly sponsored youth training programs.

Private-sector/community partnerships can be very effective in developing work-related skills in neighborhood youth. Corporations have sponsored programs both on site and in the community, frequently providing leadership, organization, and financing, as well as skilled personnel willing to work with youth. Both employers and youth gain self-esteem through working together on the project and learning new skills. In addition, the corporation has a vested interest in training these youth, who will one day enter the work force.

- **Genesis Project** (Frieda Gehlen, Ph.D., Program Director, Education and Health Care, Los Angeles Chamber of Commerce, 404 South Bixel Street, Los Angeles, CA 90017-1487 [213] 629-0620). This Employment Development Department program is a cooperative effort between youth, six inner-city schools, parents, and local employers. It works to keep young people in school while providing job opportunities or scholarships after graduation.

- **Youth Entrepreneurial Services (YES) International** (Kathleen Sullivan, 262 Grand Avenue, Suite 200, Oakland, CA 94610 [415] 893-2843): This program creates businesses owned and operated by young people. YES is a nonprofit corporation sustained by individuals, corporations, foundations, and government agencies interested in supporting an innovative response to youth unemployment. YES teaches responsible citizenship and participatory government skills while providing entrepreneurial training, business development, and counseling.

- **BUILD** (Sonny Walker, EDD Project Director, 1355 E. 114th Street, #906, Los Angeles, CA 90059 [213] 567-4552): The Employment Development Department sponsors this program, which targets the high-density unemployment community of South Central Los Angeles. Many residents there have low self-esteem because of a history of unemployment and other pressures. Project BUILD provides on-site education, job and career counseling, employment seminars, and personal counseling to help residents gain the skills and confidence necessary to break their cycle of unemployment.

References for Welfare and Self-esteem

Bane, Mary J., and D. T. Ellwood. *The Dynamics of Dependence: The Routes to Self-Sufficiency.* Cambridge, Mass.: Urban Systems Research and Engineering, 1983.

Berrueta-Clement, J. R., L. J. Schweinhart, W. S. Barnett, A. S. Epstein, and D. P. Weikart. *Changed Lives: The Effects of the Perry Preschool Program on Youth Through Age Nineteen.* Ypsilanti, Mich.: High/Scope Educational Research Foundation, 1984.

Duncan, Greg. J., and S. D. Hoffman. "The Use and Effects of Welfare: A Survey of Recent Evidence." Ann Arbor, Mich.: Institute for Social Research, University of Michigan, (Transcript), 1987.

Ellwood, D. T. "Working Off Welfare: Prospects and Policies for Self-Sufficiency of Female Family Heads." Cambridge, Mass.: John F. Kennedy School of Government, Harvard University, (Transcript), 1986.

"Investing in Our Children." New York: Child Care Action Campaign, Committee for Economic Development, 1985.

Kane, T. J. "Giving Back Control: Long-Term Poverty and Motivation," *Social Service Review*, (September, 1987), 405–419.

Kirst, Michael, et al. *Conditions of California Children.* Berkeley, Calif.: Policy Analysis for California Education, University of California, Berkeley, 1989.

Nichols-Casebolt, A. "The Psychological Effect of Income Testing Income-Support Benefits," *Social Science Review*, (June, 1986), 287–302.

Schneiderman, Leonard, Walter M. Furman, and Joseph Weber. "Self-Esteem and Chronic Welfare Dependency," in *The Social Importance of Self-Esteem.* Berkeley, Calif.: University of California Press, 1989.

Schorr, Lisbeth B., and Daniel Schorr. *Within Our Reach: Breaking the Cycle of Disadvantage and Despair.* New York: Doubleday , 1988.

The Workplace and Self-esteem

*T*he Task Force did not set out to address the issue of self-esteem in the workplace. The members found, however, that they were repeatedly challenged to do so by testimony presented at their hearings and meetings, as well as by experiences in their own lives. The members of the Task Force hope this brief presentation will open a dialogue that leads to increased esteem and responsibility at work.

Californians in many walks of life pointed out that self-esteem in the workplace is a major influence, both positively and negatively, on the six social problems the Task Force was commissioned to study. Work situations directly affect our self-esteem, income, attitudes, health, daily schedules, and access to certain resources. In turn, this directly affects the quality of our personal lives, our family life, and our children's lives.

As other sections of this report show, corporations also provide vital opportunities for training young people and exposing them to programs that promote self-esteem and personal and social responsibility. This reflects what Richard Khamsi, the secretary-treasurer of a labor union, expressed at a Task Force hearing:

> *In a nation like ours with its competitive sports, its competitive economy, its competitive educational system, we need to remind ourselves that we are members of a human community. We need to remember that we owe something to each other.*

Importance of Managerial Decisions to Self-esteem

Most companies regularly train their employees through job-related courses, seminars, and workshops. Some companies have forged beyond to offer programs that assist with drug and alcohol problems, stress reduction, physical fitness, crisis counseling, and personal growth. Employee programs such as these help create a workplace environment that nurtures self-esteem and personal and social responsibility.

The Task Force applauds the companies in California that reach out to and improve the lives of individuals in their communities. Helping, hiring, and training people demonstrates acceptance and respect for them, which helps them assume both personal and social responsibility.

In addition to its economic benefits, working hard provides many intrinsic rewards, including an affirmation of one's sense of dignity, self-reliance, and self-esteem. People work not just to make a living or to survive, but to enhance who they are as persons. Using their skills, backgrounds, and ability, individuals derive a sense of identity from the work they do; they also gain status and position in the community. Payment for labor accords the individual a certain independence and self-sufficiency, elements that nurture self-esteem.

On the other hand, certain working conditions contribute to feelings of disaffection, estrangement, frustration, and discontent. This begins at the top of the organization, according to Sharon Faret, a university professor of management who testified:

> There is absolutely no doubt in my mind that the chief executive officer and the board and the mission of any corporation set the climate and the tone, where that atmosphere can either breed fear or positive self-esteem.

Certain assumptions about human nature and human behavior lie behind every managerial decision and action. These assumptions have a profound effect on managerial attitudes and decision-making practices. Douglas MacGregor (1960) developed two categories of management theory:

Theory X: The average human being has an inherent dislike of work and will avoid it if possible. He or she, therefore, must be coerced or controlled.

Theory Y: The average human being finds expenditure of physical and mental effort in work as natural as rest or play. Under proper conditions, people seek responsibility.

MacGregor thus described in business terms the age-old debate concerning the nature of human beings. Depending on which attitude they choose, managers motivate their subordinates with either demands and threats or encouragement, appreciation, and enthusiasm.

Many companies and managers practice both attitudes to some degree. Reexamining company policies and unwritten rules to bring them into line with Theory Y helps support people's self-esteem, certainly. But like effective child rearing, managing people effectively takes more than esteem-enhancing procedures. Good business requires abundant, open communication within and across all levels of an organization, with its customers, and with its community.

Whether they are customers, employees, or community members, people who have been disenfranchised can make significant contributions to our businesses and our world. By providing access to opportunities and employment in our businesses, California companies demonstrate that they appreciate the value of each person, regardless of personal attributes or background. Human profits add to financial profits when we know that our workplaces hold all of us in esteem.

As a general rule . . . individuals need to feel good about themselves. Thus, much of what workers do and believe is in service of their self-esteem.

—Joel Brocker, in *Self-Esteem at Work*

©1986 Wernher Krutein/PHOTOVAULT

Communication Skills in the Workplace

We are not born with good communication skills, and not all of us learn them by the time we enter the workplace. This is an area in which businesses can address both productivity and social responsibility simultaneously. They can educate their employees—superiors and subordinates alike—in good communication and esteem-enhancing ways to interact and resolve problems or conflicts. This helps move us away from corporate cultures that tolerate oppressive management, politics, and competition and toward workplaces in which people appreciate and celebrate themselves, their work, and each other.

Communication skills are only one example of how we can dramatically improve our state's workplaces. Californian Tom Peters, a business philosopher and theorist, calls the business community to action in his book *Thriving in Chaos* (1987). He provides a prescription for a revolution in business. The objective is to promote the self-esteem of the individual and to make personal and social responsibility the hallmark of American business. Peters prescribes the following action:

1. Involve everyone in everything.
2. Use self-managing teams.
3. Listen, celebrate, recognize.
4. Spend time lavishly on recruiting.
5. Train and retrain.
6. Provide incentive pay for everyone.
7. Provide employment guarantees.
8. Simplify and reduce structure.
9. Reconceive the middle manager's role.
10. Eliminate bureaucratic rules and humiliating conditions.

Peters asks, "How do you humiliate and demean someone and then expect him or her to care about product quality?" The essence of our work is to ferret out all the ways in which our society sanctions the demeaning of its members and remove those practices. Peters' analysis of the workplace relates to other institutions in our society as well.

The Value of the Workplace

Positive changes in the workplace have the power to improve the day-to-day lot of the vast majority of Californians. If our dominant institutions demean their people, where are we to recruit the critical mass of esteeming, responsible human beings we need to take the thoughtful, loving, clear actions needed to prevent drug abuse, crime and violence, child and spousal abuse, the failure to learn in school, chronic welfare dependency, teen pregnancy, and other social ills? Words, deeds, and policies that harm, coerce, control, or break the spirit destroy our dignity and hope.

As important as fair wages are the noneconomic needs of workers. J. L. Wyatt (1988) writes that "organizational development studies have been showing a steady trend for more and more working people to demand job satisfaction over and above money and security . . ." These demands include recognition, participation in decision making, career mobility, and individual development. Or, as Don Albright, the division manager of a utilities company, expressed it to the Task Force:

> *Another important aspect is the employee's feeling that he or she is a part of this total effort by having an input in the decision-making process. . . . Self-esteem can be destroyed easily by superficial recognition in the form of candy-coated programs; that means recognizing people without the full knowledge of what they actually did, and you try to fool them. It can't be done. An autocratic, authoritative approach can destroy self-esteem, as well as an individual becoming embarrassed among his or her peers. . . . Too many hard and fast rules are a bugaboo for self-esteem.*

Equitable treatment is a worthy goal, but inflexible rules are not necessarily equitable. Making case-by-case decisions may take more time, but the payoff justifies this approach. It stands to reason that worker satisfaction and self-esteem improve, turnover drops, and productivity increases. The objective of the company's flexibility is to demonstrate that it values its employees (or suppliers, customers, and communities). This respect usually becomes mutual and well rooted.

Business techniques and objectives have permeated our culture and all our other major institutions—academic, military, religious, governmental, and social. According to Herzberg (1966), even international conflicts are now more a contest of relative economic and managerial strengths than a direct military challenge. The power of business to influence the society and to address societal ills is probably greater now than ever before in history.

The question at hand is how to extend the best of these techniques, resources, and problem-solving processes to promote socially responsible endeavors and to enhance workers' lives, self-esteem, and opportunities to act responsibly within their families and their communities.

Catch people in the act of doing something right.

—*Ken Blanchard,*
in *The One Minute Manager*

©1987 Wernher Krutein/PHOTOVAULT

The Importance of Child Care

Child care has become an important area for American employers to demonstrate socially responsible actions in support of American families. Given the number of working parents who must rely on others to care for their children, and the relationship between early child development and self-esteem, the availability of good child care requires serious attention from both the public and private sectors.

As employees/parents become increasingly concerned with managing the child care issue, employers have began to realize that they, too, benefit when child care problems are minimized. In a survey conducted by the Children's Council of San Francisco of Bay Area employee-sponsored child care programs, it was noted that "benefits were higher than anticipated for 93 percent of the respondents and none reported that benefits were lower than expected."

Options for employers fall into four basic categories (Silton, 1987):

1. Flexible Personnel Policies: These include alternative work schedules like flex time, compressed schedules with four days of ten hours each or three days of twelve hours each, job sharing, work at home, and parental leave policies that provide stability and support to families.
2. Financial Assistance: These include vouchers, discounts, Dependent Care Assistance Programs (DCAPS), flexible benefits plans, and charitable contributions to ongoing child care facilities or programs (like after-school programs at local schools).
3. Child Care Information Services: This approach provides information on child care through child care resource and referral networks operating in most of California's counties or by providing private assistance.
4. Direct Services to Parents: This involves the establishment of infant centers on or near the jobsite, and the provision of care to school-age children either on or near the jobsite.

Employer-sponsored child care programs can improve employee relations and corporate responsibility while also having a positive effect on recruitment, turnover, absenteeism, tardiness, productivity, and the overall well being of the workforce.

Summary to the Workplace and Self-esteem

Our businesses train and encourage employees to become leaders and managers within the workplace. Many of these individuals already volunteer their skills in community projects; and many companies encourage such efforts. This is praiseworthy, and other businesses may find their own ways to involve themselves and their employees. Just as parents have responsibilities within their families, schools, and communities, businesses exist within—and are sustained by—a system that includes individuals, social units, and governments. Company resources vary, and each business needs to exercise social responsibility in its own creative way.

Environments that recognize and respect the dignity and worth of every human being keep the human spirit intact, enhance self-esteem, and increase productivity. These human beings, then, can help others. People who work in positive and affirming environments are better able to be agents of personal and social responsibility.

Key Recommendations on the Workplace and Self-esteem

1. Encourage the development of personnel policies and working conditions that promote self-esteem and personal and social responsibility in both the private and publice sectors.
2. Public and private industry should institute policies to meet the changing needs of the American family; for example, jobsite child care, flex time work schedules, job sharing, and parental leave.

   Employers should be encouraged to implement programs, policies, and practices that ensure an esteeming environment for workers and their families.

Recommendations on the Workplace in Brief Form

1. Promote affirming workplace environments.
2. Provide employer support for employee/parents and families.
3. Encourage more businesses to get involved in their communities.

Recommendations, Discussion, and Program Examples on the Workplace and Self-esteem

<hr>

RECOMMENDATION 1

Promote affirming workplace environments.

Encourage the development of personnel policies and working conditions that promote self-esteem and personal and social responsibility in both the private and public sectors.

Employers who promote employees' responsibility and empowerment, reward quality and productivity, and build morale help not only the employees but also themselves and their agency or business. When supervisors and workers are confident of their abilities and secure in the knowledge that they are worthy human beings, and when they recognize that the same is true of others, many positive things can happen. Productivity is enhanced, mistakes can be caught, and problems can be discussed openly. Workers take new pride in their job skills and make the effort to educate themselves, improve their skills, and enhance their careers.

- **New Ways to Work** (149 Ninth St., Second floor, San Francisco, CA 94103 [415] 552-1000): This is a nonprofit work resource and research organization dedicated to assisting employers in developing more flexibility in the workplace. Their contribution to the self-esteem of workers is based on efforts to have the managers manage the work load rather than managing the people. They encourage trust, respect, and autonomy for workers through the provision of flexible work options. The organization provides publications, training, and consulting to the public and private sectors.

- **Pacific Institute's Self-Esteem Program** (1201 Western Ave., Seattle, WA 98101 [206] 628-4800): This series of video training tapes focuses on overcoming internal personal barriers to success and improving productivity among employees. Components include improving self-images, changing habits and attitudes, increasing self-awareness, building confidence, and developing social responsibility. This can be an important tool in motivating employees to take personal responsibility and map out an action plan to implement personal and career goals. The program has been successfully implemented at General Motors and Rockwell corporations.

- **The Tom Peters Group** (555 Hamilton, Ste. 201, Palo Alto, CA 94301 [415] 326-5400): This group is dedicated to excellence, with services "built around the experiences and courage of the men and women who step out to build a sustainable edge for their organizations through constant innovation, superior customer service, product quality, and consistent care and respect for the front line people who make it all happen."

Provide employer support for employee/parents and families.

Public and private industry should institute policies to meet the changing needs of the American family; for example, jobsite child care, flex time work schedules, job sharing, and parental leave.

Employers should be encouraged to implement programs, policies, and practices that ensure an esteeming environment for workers and their families.

Employers who support child care options are recognizing changes in the character of the workforce, principally in the large increase in the number of families with two wage earners. It is essential that employers be willing to identify areas of work/family conflict that affect their employees, as well as seeking solutions to ease the strain. The tension arising from having to leave children in less than acceptable situations is detrimental to the well being and self-esteem of all family members. Employee/parents need employer support to succeed both at home and at work.

- **California Child Care Resource and Referral Network** (809 Lincoln Way, San Francisco, CA 94122 [415] 566-1226): These agencies are a part of a state-wide network that helps parents find child care, document community child care needs, provide technical assistance to new and existing providers of care, and facilitate communication among existing child care service providers. It is a nonprofit public corporation representing agencies in 44 California counties.

- **California Child Care Initiative** (c/o Bank of America Foundation #3246, P. O. Box 37000, San Francisco, CA 94137 [415] 953-3175): This program, designed and managed by the Bank of America Foundation, is a public/private partnership of 33 corporations, foundations, and government to increase the supply of licensed quality child care in California. *Quality* means an esteeming environment for both the children and the providers.

In 1980, the majority of the delegates to the White House Conference on Families said flexible work hours were the most important workplace reform to help parents balance work and family.

—*The Joint Select Task Force on the Changing Family, "Planning a Family Policy for California," 1989*

Pacific Gas & Electric Co.

- **Health Enhancement Program** (Employee Assistance Program, Department of Social Services, 744 P Street, Sacramento, CA 95814 [916] 322-1329): This program promotes good health (physical, mental, emotional, and spiritual) through employee participation in activities such as weight reduction programs, Folk Dancing for Wellness, Single Parent Awareness, Narcotics Anonymous, and aerobic classes.

RECOMMENDATION 3

Encourage more businesses to get involved in their communities.

Encourage more businesses to get involved in their communities.

Given the social concerns we have today, companies are an indispensable part of the solution. What they can contribute ranges from recognition awards or meeting facilities to leadership skills to funding for educational and esteem-enhancing projects.

The business world can be of great assistance by actively supporting programs and needed legislation which contribute to the humanity of communities. Examples include: improved child care facilities, coalition programs with the local schools, mental health services, drug and alcohol prevention programs. Businesses have a great stake in the health of the communities of which they are a part and, accordingly, a significant responsibility in helping to promote healthy and esteeming communities.

- **One Small Step—United Way Coalition** (410 Bush St., San Francisco, CA 94108 [415] 722-4315): This is a coalition of business and organization leaders dedicated to increasing the number of companies which provide child care assistance to employees and their families.

References for the Workplace and Self-esteem

"Child Care, a Workforce Issue: Report of the Secretary's Task Force." Washington, D. C.: U.S. Department of Labor, April, 1988.

"Employer Supported Child Care: Options, Implementation, and Impacts." San Francisco: Children's Council of San Francisco, 1987.

Herzberg, Frederick. *Work and the Nature of Man.* New York: Thomas Y. Crowell, Co., 1966.

MacGregor, Douglas. *The Human Side of Enterprise.* New York: McGraw-Hill, 1960.

Peters, Thomas. *Thriving in Chaos.* New York: Alfred A. Knopf, 1987.

Silton, Lynn. "Child Care in the 80s," A report for the Pacific Gas and Electric Co. San Francisco: Pacific Gas and Electric Co., 1987.

Wyatt, J. L. "Work Abuse: Hidden Violence in the Workplace." Copyrighted manuscript: 492 Fair Oaks, San Francisco, CA 94110, 1988.

VII. Personal Statements

A state-wide task force needs to be representative of the whole spectrum of people within that state. We feel our Task Force fulfilled that expectation.

Even though there were only 26 of us, we included within our membership men and women of a wide range of races, ages, political and philosophical and religious perspectives, and sexual orientations.

In spite of these differences, we were amazed at the amount of good will and unanimity that we discovered over our three years together. We had open and free discussions of all issues, many positive and worthwhile compromises and respect for the dignity and worth of all persons, which is the foundation of our effort.

To make certain everyone felt that his or her special point of view was represented in this final report, the Task Force invited members to offer a brief "personal statement." Seven members accepted the invitation, and their statements follow.

Jean Barnaby

Serving on the Task Force as the designee of Senator Art Torres has been a memorable and enlightening, though sometimes frustrating, experience.

In my view, the Task Force never came fully to grips with the cultural sensitivities and qualities of the Latino community.

Appreciation of one's own ethnic and cultural heritage is a fundamental component and building block of individual self-esteem, but that consideration sometimes was lost in the accumulation of information from academic and professional behaviorists.

The final report, though much improved by the efforts of Senator Torres, has flaws. In that regard, I support the Personal Statements submitted by Task Force members William Johnson and David Shannahoff-Khalsa.

Paul Kent Froman, Ph.D.

The Task Force successfully produced its final report in spite of deep, irresolvable philosophical and theological differences among its members. Consequently, the Task Force took a strong stand against prejudice and discrimination on the basis of sexual orientation but stopped short of including Project Ten as a model program. Project Ten is committed to the support and protection of lesbian and gay youth. It saves lives and helps alleviate the pain and suffering that result from discrimination, harassment, and persecution of lesbian and gay youth.

According to the U. S. Department of Health and Human Services Task Force on Youth Suicide, over 500,000 adolescents attempt suicide each year. Over 5,000 succeed. Over 30 percent of those are lesbian and gay youth. Project Ten is desperately needed, and it needs to be replicated and expanded.

The Task Force was not mandated by the legislation to examine self-esteem and persons with AIDS, yet this is a crucial area for future study and action. This group of courageous persons is fighting for their lives in the face of a powerful and awful disease. Unfortunately, they must also fight against increased persecution and discrimination. For people with AIDS or HIV infection, self-esteem is not just a pleasant feeling, it is a life-saving, life-extending force. Appropriate and necessary counseling and other support services still fall far short of the need. Discrimination against persons with AIDS is still legal in this state.

The gay and lesbian community has been exercising its personal and social responsibility to a miraculous degree since the beginning of the AIDS crisis. I would call on the citizens of California to exercise their personal and social responsibility and demand that discrimination stop; that necessary emotional, medical, and pharmaceutical support services be provided; and that persons living with AIDS be treated, not with persecution and exclusion, but with compassion, caring, and love.

William C. Johnson, M.A.

Our final report, while worthwhile, has serious flaws. There are three areas slighted: the importance of responsibility, the significance of character development, and the value of the nuclear family.

During the tenure of the Task Force, it has proven difficult to elevate responsibility to equal standing with self-esteem. Developing self-esteem and having the character to be accountable for our own actions are interdependent. The crucial importance of all citizens having the integrity of character to be accountable for their own actions is not a concept that permeates our report. I regret that the report gives a disproportionate emphasis to self-esteem and neglects the importance of personal responsibility.

The California State Board of Education recently produced a document entitled *Moral and Civic Education and Teaching About Religion*. It's an excellent tool to help teachers learn how to teach character and better understand how self-esteem and character development are interrelated.

The family is the foundation of our society. Children's basic character and the roots of self-worth are formed within the family. The nuclear family is being devastated by divorce and separations in a transient society. The impact on individuals is catastrophic to self-esteem and social responsibility. Families need help in restoring basic values. Dealing with surface problems without reaching the roots of the cause is unproductive. I'm disappointed our report did not reach out and champion those basic values which promote individual and family responsibility.

Kenneth W. Ogden, M.Div., Ed.D.

My participation on the Task Force has brought me new insights about myself and others. I have learned much about human concern, sensitivity, and compassion. Out of the diversity of this group has come unity, and I feel that this has been demonstrated significantly in this final report.

The recommendations display a common effort to improve the conditions of Californians so that they may experience more personal satisfaction and esteem for themselves and others. These recommendations provide a vehicle for an esteeming state. I especially like the positive emphasis that is placed on the family. To strengthen this unit and the role of the parent will help create an environment where a positive self-image could be nourished.

Although the Task Force's definition of self-esteem has merit, I feel that one crucial aspect has been neglected, that being the source of a person's self-esteem. From my faith perspective, any definition that fails to recognize the eternal God as the origin of all human worth and hope is inadequate. Therefore, I would like to add to the definition:

> *Accepting myself as the image-bearer of God and the recipient of His love and forgiveness, and recognizing His centrality in my life, I appreciate my own worth and have the character to be accountable for myself and to act responsibly toward others.*

The Task Force recognizes that low self-esteem often results in costly social problems. It appears that humans have a tendency toward behavior that results in abuse to self and others as well as crime and violence. Such authorities as M. Scott Peck and Karl Menninger recognize that humans can be evil and sinful. They are not afraid to use the terms and neither should we.

For me, God in His love has provided deliverance from evil and sin through his Son, Jesus, offering forgiveness and elevating me to a state of esteem that I could not achieve within myself. God makes this same gift available to you—a positive basis for self-esteem.

Eunice Sato, M.A.

One of the clearest messages I get from this Task Force report is that a profound generation gap exists between the majority of Task Force members (who were children of the sixties era) and a minority of us who are older. We older Task Force members believe profoundly in the existence and importance of moral absolutes while the younger majority is content with moral relativism. I strongly disagree with the moral relativism that pervades the Task Force report. After serving on the Task Force for three years, I am convinced more then ever that strong moral values are the key to self-esteem.

Self-esteem and strength of character go hand in hand. Strength of character is rooted in self-knowledge. The most profound sort of self-knowledge concerns principles that guide us through our lives: our moral values. In order for people to get along with one another, the fundamental moral values cannot be matters of relativistic free choice; rather, they must be held in common. Our social institutions—family, school, church, government, and all others—have the important task of passing on our commonly held values. The Task Force report minimizes not only the importance of our commonly held values, but the importance of ensuring that our institutions adequately fulfill their function as beacons of morality.

When people stand for strong moral values, they have a strong sense of self in the most profound and important sense. Thus, they cannot help but have self-esteem. Moral values help us aim high not only for ourselves but for our society as well. The prime focus of the Task Force report should be on strategies for making our society more morally strong and morally aware. By stressing moral relativism, the report undermines rather than enhances self-esteem.

Policies and recommendations for building self-esteem which ignore the fundamental moral dimension of character education will not solve such skyrocketing social problems as crime, drug or child abuse, teenage pregnancy, or chronic dependency.

The best case in point is teen pregnancy. The word abstinence is mentioned in the Task Force report, but the entire argument in the supporting text expresses no normative value preference for abstinence over sexual activity. The report does not offer any recognition of what is undoubtedly the truth of the matter—namely, that teens with the highest self-esteem will choose abstinence. Instead, the report legitimizes sexually active behavior. Such a supposedly "value-free" policy will worsen the problem of teenage pregnancies and its side effects.

David Shannahoff-Khalsa

My views and experience are so substantially different from the group consensus that I am compelled to address four areas of major discrepancy.

1. The Task Force's interpretation of the UC professors' academic findings understates the absence of a significant linkage of self-esteem and the six social problems. Quoting Professor Smelser's overview (p. 15), "The news most consistently reported is that the associations between self-esteem and its expected consequences are mixed, insignificant, or absent."

2. I disagree with the content of the "Principles" document as an effective solution for these social problems. Principles alone will not provide solutions for those in need. Techniques or therapies

for reducing the common problems of anger, fear, stress, tension, anxiety, addictions, dyslexias, and obsessive-compulsive disorders have all been overlooked. The "Principles" document is simplistic, lacks the "how to," and is of little use.

3. The attention given to the role of the mind and mental development, especially the subconscious mind, as a factor in the development of healthy self-esteem is virtually absent. Why we have not managed to abide by codes of conduct, values, or commandments is not adequately addressed. Without probing the depths one will never reach the heights.

4. Healthy self-esteem is a derivative of living with the basic virtues of kindness, righteousness, organization, courage, and grace. Self-esteem cannot be administered, injected, or given to anyone. It is a by-product, no more central to living than happiness or dignity. This elusive term describing ones feelings of self is being promoted as a universal remedy for a society that has become increasingly complex and dysfunctional. Such an approach ignores what may seem to be the more difficult remedies that pertain to man's consciousness, intelligence, and intuition.

Lynn Silton, M.S.

I feel we need to be tough on institutions, not teens. With reference to the Task Force's recommendation on juvenile justice, it is not our message to encourage jailing, detention, or other harsh punishment for the children of California—who cannot vote, have few personal resources, and depend on parents and society to protect them.

Our report actually investigates kids' environments, and the relationship between failure and delinquency and offending institutional, parenting, and family practices.

Our idea is that kids who break the law can gain new respect for themselves and their society by performing the kind of community service work that strengthens the heart, not cracks it—work like helping the elderly, beautifying parks, helping the homeless. In short, we want to provide opportunities not available or encouraged in their normal environments. Our idea is that our institutions need to accept responsibility for the results of their choices before our youth can be expected to follow suit.

VIII. Conclusion

Concurrent with the completion of this report, all of Eastern Europe has broken loose with people's revolutions—toppling restrictive governments, creating new human possibilities, facilitating personal and social relationships, demanding democracy. This, we feel, is of the very essence of the self-esteem and personal and social responsibility endeavor.

Every individual human being deserves to be treated with dignity and respect. Governments must recognize the inherent worth in being human. So must communities, businesses, schools, families. And, perhaps most importantly of all, each of us must recognize and nurture this truth about ourselves. When we build our lives around an accurate and appropriate appreciation of our own worth as human beings, persons who are capable of dealing with life and worthy of dignity and respect just because we are human, then we are most productive, most caring and responsible in our relationships with others, and most fulfilled within ourselves.

This is not a new understanding. In many ways it was basic to the founding of this nation. And yet, it is a truth we need desperately to re-learn. Perhaps, by its very nature it is a fundamental truth that must be understood anew by every person, interpreted and implemented anew in every generation. As T. S. Eliot wrote in his poem "Little Gidding":

> We shall not cease from exploration
> and the end of all our exploring
> will be to arrive where we started

As fellow pilgrims, we wish you well on your journey. May we learn and grow in such a way as to offer assistance, encouragement, and friendship to all who share the journey with us.

This movement gives substance to the dream for freedom and responsibility which lives in the heart of each person.

—*Eunice Sato*
Japanese/American Task Force member

R91-02 (Fourth printing) 003-0025-91 300 8M